ENDANGERED AND DISAPPEARING
BIRDS
OF THE
MIDWEST

Matt Williams

Indiana University Press

This book is a publication of

Indiana University Press
Office of Scholarly Publishing
Herman B Wells Library 350
1320 East 10th Street
Bloomington, Indiana 47405 USA

iupress.indiana.edu

© 2018 by Matt Williams

Manufactured in the United States of America

Library of Congress Cataloging-in-Publication Data

Names: Williams, Matt (Photographer), author.
Title: Endangered and disappearing birds of
    the Midwest / Matt Williams.
Other titles: Birds of the Midwest
Description: Bloomington, Indiana : Indiana University
    Press, [2018] | Includes bibliographical references.
Identifiers: LCCN 2018015000 (print) | LCCN 2018016443
    (ebook) | ISBN 9780253035318 (e-book) |
    ISBN 9780253035271 (h : alk. paper)
Subjects: LCSH: Birds—Middle West—Identification. |
    Birds—Middle West—Pictorial works. | Rare birds—
    Middle West—Identification. | Rare birds—Middle West—
    Pictorial works. | Endangered species—Middle West.
Classification: LCC QL683.M55 (ebook) | LCC QL683.
    M55 W55 2018 (print) | DDC 598.0977—dc23
LC record available at https://lccn.loc.gov/2018015000

1 2 3 4 5   23 22 21 20 19 18

CONTENTS

ACKNOWLEDGMENTS

I'd like to thank Richard Urbanek, Dave Ewert, Amy Kearns, and Francesca Cuthbert for their contributions to this work. Their deep knowledge and expertise adds much to the quality of this book; it truly was a privilege to work with each of them. Thanks also to Dave for helping me locate good places in northern Michigan to photograph several species I was missing. In addition, I need to thank Ken Brock, Don Gorney, and John Kendall, who each provided comments that strengthened a number of the captions in the book giving details on the birds shown. If any errors remain, they are mine and not theirs.

Thanks also to my family for their encouragement, patience, and support. My parents and grandparents instilled in me a love of birds and nature, and my wife and children have shared that love with me and given me the time and freedom to pursue time-consuming projects like this one! I love you all more deeply than I can put into words.

Matt Williams
Genesis 1:20–22

LIST OF COMMONLY USED ABBREVIATIONS

AOU   American Ornithological Union

IUCN   International Union for Conservation of Nature

NABCI   North American Bird Conservation Initiative

PIF   Partners in Flight

USFWS   United States Fish and Wildlife Service

USGS   United States Geological Survey

WHSRN   Western Hemisphere Shorebird Reserve Network

ENDANGERED AND DISAPPEARING
BIRDS OF THE MIDWEST

Introduction

Birds are some of the most beautiful, engaging creatures on Earth. From the songbirds that wake us up in the morning with their dawn chorus to the birds that flock to our backyard feeders and brighten a gloomy winter day, birds are enjoyed by millions of people across our planet. Their bright colors, cheerful songs, and interesting behaviors fascinate us, while the ecosystem services they provide may be more important than we realized.

Simply by going about their daily lives, birds help control outbreaks of destructive caterpillars and other insects, disperse seeds to new areas, pollinate crops, dispose of carcasses that could otherwise spread disease, and keep rodent populations in check. In one study of coffee plantations in Guatemala, it was estimated that birds reduced the populations of pest insects enough to increase farm profits by $126 per acre per year. In Pakistan, another study found that birds were even more effective than pesticides at controlling tick populations that were responsible for reducing milk production in local dairy herds. In another example, a decline in vulture populations in India was tied to disease outbreaks that led to the death of more than forty thousand people and increased health-care costs by $34 billion over a fourteen-year period.

Examples of the ecosystem services of birds are numerous, and we are really just beginning to understand the full impacts that birds have. However, birds benefit people in other ways as well. Birdwatching is one of the most popular outdoor hobbies in the United States. A 2012 survey by the U.S. Fish and Wildlife Service reports more than 46 million Americans identify themselves as birdwatchers. This group spends an estimated $4 billion annually on birdseed, $12 billion on travel, and roughly $24 billion on binoculars, spotting scopes, birdhouses, and other gear. These are dollars that are pumped into our economy every year, and all this spending employs 671,000 people.

And yet for all their beauty, for all the ecosystem services they provide, for all the financial benefits that come to our economy from the millions of people who are passionate about birdwatching, many of our populations of birds are declining. Simply put, many bird species across the Midwest, and the country, are in serious trouble.

Loss of habitat to agriculture and energy expansion, collisions with vehicles and structures, encounters with feral cats, changing forest conditions, climate change, and other threats all likely play a role in bird population declines. Using USGS North American Breeding Bird Survey data and other information, the 2016 Partners in Flight Landbird Conservation Plan states that nearly 20 percent of all North American landbird species are on a path to becoming endangered and/or extinct without conservation action. In the past 50 years alone, more than one-third of our bird species have declined by at least 15 percent, with many suffering declines of more than 70 percent. In total, these declines add up to a loss of 1.5 billion individual birds in just five decades. What a stunning loss.

The goal of this book is to highlight forty species of birds that winter, breed, or migrate through the Midwest and are in trouble because of either a dangerously small population size or rapid population declines in recent decades. Some species in this book may still be quite common, but they are listed in these pages because steep declines in recent years put their future in doubt. Others' populations may actually have grown recently, but the overall population size remains small enough that their survival remains tenuous. By no means is this book meant to be a complete list of all at-risk species in the Midwest; rather, it is a representative sample of some of the most beautiful and interesting birds from our region that may be lost at some point in the future unless significant work is undertaken to mitigate existing threats to these species and ensure that sufficient high-quality habitat in all phases of the birds' life cycles remains. My hope is that this book inspires a commitment and dedication among many to ensure that we all take appropriate steps to protect and preserve these species for future generations to be thrilled by.

1

Northern Bobwhite
(*Colinus virginianus*)

STATUS:

Common Bird in Steep Decline, IUCN Near
Threatened, State Special Concern (Ohio)

ESTIMATED POPULATION TREND:

–85% during the period 1966–2014

LENGTH: 9–10"

Northern Bobwhite, April, Texas: Male Northern Bobwhites have a
strong black-and-white pattern that marks the face, and heavy speckling
on the breast and scaling on the back that provides camouflage.

■ Year-round

Species Account. From the 1950s through the early 1970s, the Northern Bobwhite, or Bobwhite Quail, enjoyed robust population numbers across much of the Midwest. During this time period, 150,000 hunters annually killed as many as 2.5 million quail in the state of Illinois alone. However, by the 2015–2016 quail season in Illinois, 7,665 hunters harvested only 29,674 birds—an indication of how quail populations have fared across the Midwest as a whole in recent decades.

Another measure of the quail population is through calling routes. Quail calling routes are run each summer by biologists working for several Midwestern states. In Illinois, the routes are run in prime quail habitat twice per year—once during the period May 10–June 10, and a second time from June 10 to July 10. There are twenty

Northern Bobwhite, April, Texas: The female Northern Bobwhite is patterned similarly to the male but is less strikingly colored.

stops on the route and observers record the number of quail heard or seen during three minutes of observation at each stop. The 2016 numbers revealed that quail were recorded at only 24 percent of the stops, which marked the third year in a row that the numbers declined, representing a 6 percent decrease from the previous year's results.

Although quail numbers fluctuate substantially from year to year, similar population drops since the early 1970s have taken place across the region, and some Midwestern states like Indiana even closed the quail season for a number of years in an effort to help the population rebound. Many biologists and hunters point to the harsh winters of the late 1970s as a turning point in quail numbers. In winters with below-normal temperatures and heavy snow cover, quail numbers crash. On bitterly cold winter nights, quail coveys huddle together in a circle facing outward, with each body touching another in order to stay warm. However, in extreme temperatures, entire coveys may freeze or die of starvation if they are unable to find food in deep snow. In the late 1970s, there were three such winters in a row in the Midwest, and population numbers have still not recovered. Other factors are likely in play as well—for example, the intensification of agriculture is often cited as a reason for the decline of Northern Bobwhite numbers. Fewer fencerows, increasing use of chemicals to control insect populations, fewer fallow, brushy fields, and mowing during the nesting season all likely play a part in the overall decline.

Endangered and Disappearing Birds of the Midwest

Because of its popularity among hunters, the Northern Bobwhite is a highly studied bird. Genetics studies have identified twenty-two separate subspecies throughout the bird's range. Other studies have looked at the foods eaten by these small quail. In examining the stomach contents of over eight hundred Northern Bobwhites, nearly seventy different kinds of food items were identified over the course of one two-year study. Some of the most common fall foods were corn, sassafras, ragweed, insects, wheat, acorns, and foxtail.

Although the current situation seems a little bleak for these beautiful birds, there is some good news. Bobwhite populations farther south, where winters are warmer, seem to be doing better than they are in the Midwest. Also, hunters and groups like Quail Forever are working hard to improve habitat across the core of the birds' range. Programs for farmers, such as the Conservation Reserve Program, are also important opportunities to increase the amount of suitable habitat for these birds.

Identification. The male is a chunky quail. In the Midwest, male birds have a *rufous band* across their breast that continues onto their backs. The head is striking, with a *bright white throat* and a *white stripe that runs over the eye* and down the nape. This contrasts with a black beak and a black stripe through the eye. The back is mottled with tan, gray, and black. Females have a similar appearance but have muted buff on the head, whereas the male is bright white. In the Midwest, the Northern Bobwhite is fairly unmistakable, with the possible exception of being confused with a young pheasant or Wild Turkey.

Vocalizations. The Northern Bobwhite says its name *bob-WHITE*—often from a fencepost or a dead branch. The call is a clear, two-part whistle, with the second note emphasized and slurring upward in pitch. Occasionally, the call will have three notes instead of two, with a second *bob* note slightly higher than the first. The birds also have a variety of calls used to stay in touch with other members of their covey. Some of these calls warn of danger, with a different call used for ground-based predators than for aerial threats.

Nesting. Northern Bobwhites can lay anywhere from twelve to sixteen eggs per nest attempt, with as many as an incredible twenty-eight reported in some cases. The nest is a shallow scrape on the ground, usually sheltered by a shrub or clump of grass. Nests are usually located within sixty-five feet of a field edge or a road. Chicks leave the nest upon hatching and may be tended by either parent. The adults will flutter or drag a wing in an effort to distract predators away from the chicks.

Matt Williams

2

Greater Prairie-Chicken
(*Tympanuchus cupido*)

STATUS:

NABCI 2016 Watch List, 2016 PIF Watch List, IUCN
Vulnerable, State Special Concern (Minnesota), State
Threatened (Wisconsin), and State Endangered (Illinois)

ESTIMATED POPULATION TREND:

>−50% during the period 1970–2014

LENGTH: 17"

Greater Prairie-Chicken, April, Illinois: The male Greater Prairie-Chickens
perform on the lek for females by inflating bright-orange air sacs on the
sides of their necks, and then forcing the air back out to make a hollow,
"booming" noise while quickly stomping their feet at the same time.

Year-round

Year-round (historic)

Species Account. At first light in the early spring, male Greater Prairie-Chickens gather on traditional leks—places of short grass often on a small rise in the prairie where the birds can see a good distance. Here, they stake out and defend small territories against anywhere from a handful to as many as several dozen other males. They erect pinnae feathers over their heads almost like feathered horns, revealing orange air sacs on the side of their necks. The birds can inflate these sacs, then force the air back out to create a hollow moaning, or "booming," noise that can carry for great distances on a still morning. The booming is also often accompanied by a foot-stomping display in which the males rapidly stomp their feet while holding their tails erect and wings stiffly at their sides. In addition to booming, the birds cackle and whoop as they square off head-to-head on the lek. Sometimes fighting males leap into the air and beat each other with their wings while attempting to scratch at their opponent with their sharp claws. This amazing cacophony of sound reaches a crescendo when a female bird approaches the lek. Hens calmly and slowly walk around the lek, feeding and often appearing disinterested in the fierce battles taking place around them. Typically, only the most dominant one or two males do the great majority of the breeding, which is the reason for the battles. As the morning wears on, males will slowly wander off the lek or sometimes they fly off together in groups, only to resume their hostilities at full tilt the next day.

Historically, Greater Prairie-Chickens were abundant in this country. They ranged across the midsection of the nation, from Canada to Mexico. A subspecies of the Greater Prairie-Chicken known as the Heath Hen bred as far east as the East Coast and was so numerous it was called "poor man's food" because they were so cheap and plentiful. Some have even speculated that it was Heath Hen that was eaten at the first Thanksgiving. Despite this abundance, probably because of overhunting and a loss of habitat, among other factors, the last Heath Hen died on Martha's Vineyard in 1932.

A second subspecies known as the Attwater's Prairie-Chicken is found only along the coastal prairies of southeastern Texas. As recently as 1900, these birds may have numbered as high as 1 million in the coastal prairies stretching from Louisiana to Mexico. Despite captive breeding and other efforts, these birds are now critically endangered, and the total wild population may hover around one hundred birds.

In the Midwest, Greater Prairie-Chickens have also suffered significant declines from their peak population numbers. Although the birds were once present in large numbers in every Midwestern state, today they are completely gone from Michigan, Indiana, and Ohio, and they hang on only in small numbers in Iowa, Illinois, and Wisconsin. In our region, only Minnesota boasts a population of reasonable size, with estimates of several thousand males in the northwest part of the state being recorded in censuses of the leks. Although other factors have played a role, habitat loss is likely the biggest reason for the decline of the Greater Prairie-Chicken, with only about 1 percent of native prairie habitat remaining in the Midwest. The birds need thousands of acres of intact prairie with few trees for avian predators to perch in. With so little of this type of habitat remaining, it is not hard to see why we have so few birds left today.

Fortunately, Greater Prairie-Chickens remain in good numbers outside the Midwest across portions of Kansas, Nebraska, and South Dakota, where swaths of native prairie habitat still exist. Overall, the birds appear to be doing quite well in these states, with a total population estimated at over four hundred thousand. Efforts are under way to translocate some of these birds to the Midwest in an attempt to vary the gene pool of the remaining small, isolated populations in order to stabilize and grow them before they disappear.

Greater Prairie-Chicken, April, Illinois: Two male Greater Prairie-Chickens square off on the lek. Fights can be intense, and they determine dominance on the lek. Many of the birds in Illinois have been a part of the translocation program to increase genetic diversity and bear either silver or colored leg bands to aid researchers.

Identification. Greater Prairie-Chickens are relatively *large, stocky chickenlike birds*. They are *heavily striped* and show a chocolate brown tail. The male's orange air sacs are usually visible only during breeding displays. In flight, the birds show rounded wings and frequently glide before settling back into the grass. The Sharp-tailed Grouse is similar looking, but it is more spotted than striped and has a pointed tail rather than the short, stubby tail of the Greater Prairie-Chicken.

Vocalizations. Away from the booming grounds, the birds are typically quite quiet, although they may give a few short cackles if flushed. Vocalizations on the lek include cackles, whoops, and the low, hollow moaning sound known as booming.

Nesting. The male takes no part in nesting or brood rearing. Hens typically lay between ten and twelve eggs that are light buff and speckled with brown. Incubation lasts approximately three weeks, and the chicks leave the nest and can forage for their own food immediately after hatching.

Matt Williams

Greater Prairie-Chicken, April, Illinois: A hen slowly walks through the lek, being courted by various males in full display.

3

Yellow-billed Cuckoo
(*Coccyzus americanus*)

STATUS:
Common Bird in Steep Decline

ESTIMATED POPULATION TREND:
−52% during the period 1966–2015

LENGTH: 11"

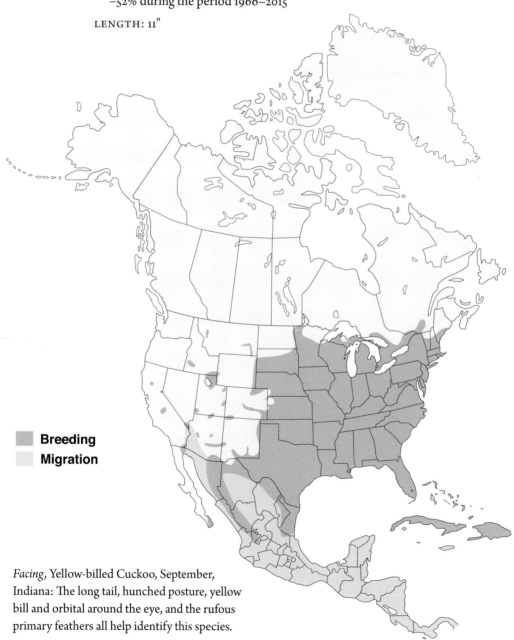

■ **Breeding**
■ **Migration**

Facing, Yellow-billed Cuckoo, September,
Indiana: The long tail, hunched posture, yellow
bill and orbital around the eye, and the rufous
primary feathers all help identify this species.

Species Account. The bird sits hunched in the shadows, its body and long tail completely motionless. Slowly, very slowly, it turns its head to look first up, then down. Slow as a sloth, the bird cranes its neck to peer carefully at every leaf surface in all directions. The bird is a Yellow-billed Cuckoo, and it is hunting. It is patiently watching for any sign of movement that would betray the location of a tasty caterpillar in the nearby foliage. Finally satisfied that no meals are within easy reach, the cuckoo takes flight and heads deeper into the forest. After having sat motionless for so long, the swiftness and directness of its flight is breathtaking: it flies with swept-back wings and its long tail streaming behind it, twisting to avoid branches in its path and flashing red primary feathers as it disappears.

Because of their habit of sitting motionless for long periods, cuckoos can be remarkably difficult to spot despite their relatively large size. Often, the best way to find them is to listen for their unique, rhythmic knocking call. According to some, cuckoos give these calls more often on cloudy days or in response to thunder, which has given rise to their nickname—the rain crow. The nesting season for cuckoos in the Midwest can last all the way through early September, making them one of the few birds still calling during the dog days of late summer.

Cuckoos are beneficial in helping to control populations of insects. One of the few birds that eat hairy caterpillars, cuckoos have been reported to eat as many as one hundred tent caterpillars in one meal. In fact, outbreaks of tent caterpillars or gypsy moths often result in higher numbers of cuckoos in the area, and food-supply levels may even affect the timing of the breeding season. In addition to caterpillars, Yellow-billed Cuckoos also eat spiders, katydids, and cicadas. They have even been observed flying to the ground to take crickets, grasshoppers, and other prey as large as small frogs.

Yellow-billed Cuckoos have been known to occasionally lay their eggs in other birds' nests. During times of high food abundance, female cuckoos will lay their eggs in another cuckoo's nest, as well as in the nests of American Robins, Wood Thrushes, and Gray Catbirds. If food is especially scarce, the adults may remove the youngest nestling from their own nest in order to give a higher chance of survival to the larger chicks.

The Yellow-billed Cuckoo has a wide distribution in North America, with birds occurring from the East Coast to California. However, the cuckoo has suffered a significant population decline from its historical levels. The birds have been extirpated from British Columbia, Washington, Oregon, and Nevada. In California, the population has gone from an estimated fifteen thousand pairs to forty pairs in the past hundred years. Because of these declines, the Yellow-billed Cuckoo population west of the Rocky Mountains has been granted protection as a federally threatened species under the Endangered Species Act. In the Midwest, the Yellow-billed Cuckoo is still a relatively

Yellow-billed Cuckoo, May, Indiana: Yellow-billed Cuckoos show significant amounts of yellow on the bill, especially on the lower mandible.

common bird in forested habitat, where it prefers early successional young forest with plenty of scrubby, brushy areas. However, even in the Midwest, cuckoo numbers have fallen dramatically since the 1960s. The declines are primarily due to habitat loss, with estimated population drops of 70 percent in Minnesota and Iowa, and more than 80 percent in Indiana.

Identification. The Yellow-billed Cuckoo is a relatively large, slender bird about the size of a robin, but *with a long tail with obvious white spots* that are most noticeable on the underside. The bird has a yellow eye ring and a plain brown back, with clean, unmarked white underparts. The wings are brown *with rufous primary feathers*. The bill is *heavy and large, and is primarily yellow*, with some black on the top mandible. The Black-billed Cuckoo appears quite similar but has red around the eye instead of yellow, a smaller all-black bill, and smaller white tail spots.

Vocalizations. The call is a loud, hollow, *tick tick tick tick tick, kowlp kowlp kowlp*. The *tick* notes are rapid and all on one pitch, while the *kowlp* notes descend in pitch and are a little more drawn out. The birds also make a cooing call at times that sounds almost like that of a pigeon. Yellow-billed Cuckoos have been known to call even at night during the breeding season.

Nesting. Yellow-billed Cuckoos have been found to nest anywhere from two to thirty feet or more aboveground. Trees used commonly for nesting include elm, hawthorn, and locust, and trees that are overgrown with wild grapevines or other tangles of vegetation seem to be favorable sites for the rather flimsy, platform nests. Typical clutch size is from two to three eggs, with as many as five to six possible.

Matt Williams

Facing, Yellow-billed Cuckoo, May, Indiana: Seen from underneath, the tail shows large white spots.

4

Black-billed Cuckoo
(*Coccyzus erythropthalmus*)

STATUS:
   2014 NABCI Yellow Watch List, 2016 NABCI Watch List,
   2016 PIF Watch List, State Threatened (Illinois)

ESTIMATED POPULATION TREND:
   –66% during the period 1966–2015

LENGTH: 11.5"

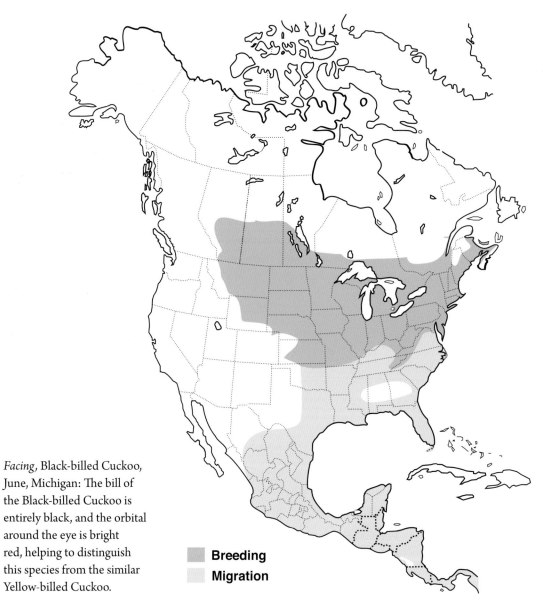

Facing, Black-billed Cuckoo, June, Michigan: The bill of the Black-billed Cuckoo is entirely black, and the orbital around the eye is bright red, helping to distinguish this species from the similar Yellow-billed Cuckoo.

Breeding
Migration

Species Account. Like the similar Yellow-billed Cuckoo, Black-billed Cuckoos sit for long periods with very little movement and heads tilted to search for prey. They typically stay concealed in the foliage and are more often heard than seen. The birds will call during daylight hours, but during the breeding season, Black-billed Cuckoos call even at night. Night calling is most frequent between the hours of 8 p.m. and midnight, and calls are often given while the bird is in flight over the breeding grounds—as often as ten times or more per hour. This active behavior at night along with sluggish behavior during the day, has led some to suggest that Black-billed Cuckoos may be nocturnal during the breeding season.

Breeding habitat for the Black-billed Cuckoo consists of open areas such as old fields, interspersed with groves of aspen or other young deciduous forest or mixed deciduous-coniferous forest patches. Shelterbelts and orchards are also used by these birds, as are other shrubby areas, especially along the edges of rivers or wetlands. The habitat needs on the wintering ground are poorly understood for this species, but birds have been recorded in Colombia, western Venezuela, Peru, Bolivia, and Ecuador.

Black-billed Cuckoos are voracious predators of several species of destructive caterpillar, including tent caterpillars, and gypsy moth larvae. The birds tear open the nests of caterpillars to feed or pluck caterpillars from branches or leaves. Prey also includes cicadas, grasshoppers, and weevils. When captured, prey is often beat on a branch or rolled in the bill to subdue it, or possibly to remove the spines of some caterpillars. Spines that are not removed will pierce the stomach lining of the cuckoos and remain there, giving the stomach a fuzzy appearance. Black-billed Cuckoos have the amazing ability to cough up the stomach lining as a pellet if embedded caterpillar spines become too numerous.

In the past, great numbers of cuckoos were reported to occur in areas where there were large caterpillar outbreaks. Now, however, it is rare to see more than one or two birds together at a time. Black-billed Cuckoos respond to large outbreaks of caterpillars by timing their nesting around these events and by increasing the number of eggs laid during periods of high prey availability. As pesticides have been used more frequently to control outbreaks of destructive caterpillar species, though, it is likely that cuckoo numbers have also dropped as their prey has become less numerous. Some evidence also suggests that cuckoos may be accumulating some of the toxins from pesticides used to control caterpillar outbreaks. One study indicated that large numbers of dead cuckoos in Nova Scotia may have been from arsenical pesticides used to treat caterpil-

Facing, Black-billed Cuckoo, June, Michigan: Although more
common in groves of young aspen or other deciduous trees,
Black-billed Cuckoos also occur in stands of young evergreens.

Endangered and Disappearing Birds of the Midwest

lar outbreaks in orchards there. Other potential causes for their recent declines include the removal of many fencerow habitats from agricultural areas, a drop in the acreage of orchards, and collisions during migration with towers and tall buildings.

Identification. The Black-billed Cuckoo is a *slim, long-tailed bird with a plain brown back and white underparts.* The black bill is relatively thick and sturdy with a slight downward curve. The underside of the tail appears grayish with *narrow white spots.* Adult birds have a red eye ring. The similar Yellow-billed Cuckoo has much larger white spots on the underside of the tail, reddish coloration on the wings, a yellow instead of red eye ring, and a yellow lower mandible instead of one that is all black.

Vocalizations. The *cu-cu-cu-cu* notes are quickly repeated two to five times all on one pitch, with a tonal quality that is similar to that of the Mourning Dove. Black-billed Cuckoos can also make whimpering calls and harsher-sounding cackles that are similar to the vocalizations of the Yellow-billed Cuckoo.

Nesting. Like other cuckoos, the Black-billed Cuckoo occasionally lays its eggs in the nests of other species, such as Northern Cardinals, Chipping Sparrows, Gray Catbirds, Wood Thrushes, and other cuckoos. Depending on prey availability, they may lay two to five or more blue-green eggs. The nest is a loose platform of sticks, usually in dense vegetation within ten feet of the ground. Incubation of the eggs is done by both the male and the female. Within a few hours of hatching, the young are quite mobile, and they may leave the nest within a week. When frightened, the young may freeze with the neck outstretched similar to the American Bittern's strategy to avoid detection.

Matt Williams

Facing, Black-billed Cuckoo, June, Michigan:
The underside of the tail has white spots, but
they are not as bright or as large as the spots
on the tail of Yellow-billed Cuckoos.

Whooping Crane
(*Grus americana*)

5

STATUS:

2014 NABCI Red Watch List, 2016 NABCI Watch List,
Federally Endangered, IUCN Endangered,
State Endangered (Indiana)

ESTIMATED POPULATION TREND:

Approximately tenfold increase from 43 to >400
during the period 1966–2016

LENGTH: 59"

Whooping Cranes, December, Indiana: In flight, Whooping
Cranes show black wing tips on their otherwise white bodies.
Several of the birds in this photo are color banded or have
transmitters to help biologists track their movements.

Breeding
Winter
Year-round

Species Account. The Whooping Crane, at a height of up to five feet, is the tallest bird in North America. Adults have conspicuous white plumage with black primaries. The name comes from the whooping call, which is produced with the aid of a five-foot-long trachea coiled in the sternum and can be heard miles away. Although not common since European settlement, Whooping Cranes were formerly widespread across a breeding range including wetlands of the north-central United States, the prairie provinces of Canada, and a few additional North American locations. Wintering birds were located mainly in southern Texas and Louisiana and at scattered other locations in the southern United States and Mexico. By 1942, mainly because of the draining of wetland habitat for agriculture as well as indiscriminate shooting, the species was reduced to a small flock of fifteen to sixteen migratory individuals wintering at Aransas National Wildlife Refuge on the Gulf Coast of Texas and six individuals in a nonmigratory flock at White Lake, Louisiana. The Louisiana population did not survive. In 1954 the remote breeding grounds of the birds wintering at Aransas were discovered in Wood

Buffalo National Park in the Northwest Territories of Canada. All Whooping Cranes alive today are descendants of that small remnant flock.

The Aransas–Wood Buffalo population begins spring migration in late March or April and nesting in late April or May. Fall migration begins in mid-September, with arrival at Aransas in late October or November. Whooping Cranes in the reintroduced eastern migratory population (EMP) usually depart wintering areas ranging from Indiana to Florida in March. Nesting in Wisconsin usually begins in April, with renesting occurring through May. The Whooping Crane incubation period is thirty days. Chicks usually fledge in eighty to ninety days. Migration of the EMP to wintering areas usually begins in November. Birds in Louisiana nest between February and May.

Whooping Cranes are much more carnivorous than Sandhill Cranes and feed on small aquatic animals of all types: fish, frogs, mussels, crayfish, crabs (their predominant food at Aransas), and other invertebrates. Whooping Cranes also feed on berries and acorns. During migration and wintering, waste grain, especially corn, in harvested fields is a staple food.

Approximately 150 Whooping Cranes are held at five propagation facilities and at seven display locations. These facilities protect the species from extinction and provide a source of stock for reintroductions. Reintroductions attempted in the Rocky Mountains (begun 1975) and central Florida (begun 1993) were unsuccessful and have been discontinued (fifteen birds remained in the Florida population as of 2016). The third reintroduction attempt began in central Wisconsin in 2001, attained one hundred individuals in 2010, and as of 2016 remained at approximately that level. Initially, the population wintered mainly in Florida, but in recent years the winter distribution has been scattered, with the greatest concentrations in southwestern Indiana and northern Alabama. Survival, migration, breeding-pair formation, and territory establishment have been largely successful, but nest desertion and chick mortality problems have precluded adequate reproduction to sustain the population. Proposed solutions to the latter two problems remain controversial. A fourth reintroduction began in southwestern Louisiana with initial releases in 2011 to establish a nonmigratory population. The first chick fledged in 2016; that flock contained fifty-nine individuals at the end of that year. To date, none of the reintroductions has resulted in self-sustaining populations.

Identification. Adults are *white with black primaries.* Juveniles are light brown mottled with white, and they molt into adult plumage during the first winter. Body silhouette is similar to the much more common Sandhill Crane. In flight, Whooping Cranes may sometimes be confused with Sandhill Cranes, White Pelicans, and Snow Geese.

Vocalizations. The unison call is given synchronously by territorial pairs. The male and female parts of the call are also frequently given by lone territorial or assertive birds. Another loud call is the alarm (guard) call; several other calls, such as the brood call, are low in volume.

Nesting. The flat-topped nest is about three to four feet in diameter and built from dead herbaceous vegetation that is piled in an open wetland. Typically two eggs, but sometimes only one, are laid. Eggs are light olive brown with darker brown blotches. Females and males trade incubation duties. Young leave the nest and follow the parents shortly after hatching. Both parents feed the young, and the female mainly broods them at night, often on a brooding platform constructed by the parents.

Richard Urbanek

6

Piping Plover
(*Charadrius melodus*)

STATUS:

(Great Lakes population) 2014 NABCI Red Watch List, 2016
NABCI Watch List, Federally Endangered, IUCN Near Threatened,
State Endangered (Michigan, Ohio, Indiana, Illinois, Iowa, Wisconsin)

ESTIMATED POPULATION TREND:

Initially a decline until after federal listing; in response to intensive
management and protection the overall trend has been a population
increase during the period 1986–2016.

LENGTH: 7"

Piping Plover, January, Louisiana: In basic plumage,
Piping Plovers have orange legs, all black beaks, and
appear a soft, muted gray and white overall.

Breeding
Nonbreeding

Species Account. The Great Lakes population of Piping Plovers has never been large. It has been estimated at as high as eight hundred pairs and as low as three hundred to four hundred pairs in the late 1800s to early 1900s. In 2016, seventy-five pairs nested along the shoreline of four states (Michigan, Wisconsin, Illinois, New York) and Ontario. This number represents about a fourfold increase since listing, and their range has also expanded from its initial contraction in the mid-1980s. Great Lakes Piping Plovers represent one of three populations in North America. The other two, Northern Great Plains and Prairie Canada, as well as Atlantic Coast (including Canada's Maritime Provinces), are considerably larger; they are each estimated at more than two thousand pairs. Piping Plovers nest only in North America and are considered one of

Piping Plover, January, Louisiana: This photograph gives a nice comparison between a Piping Plover on the right and a Semipalmated Plover on the left. The Semipalmated Plover has a much richer brown color on the back, while the Piping Plover appears very pale in comparison. This Piping Plover was banded as a chick along the Missouri River in South Dakota by researchers from Virginia Tech.

the continent's most imperiled shorebird species. They are listed as endangered in the Great Lakes and threatened in the other two populations. Reasons for decline in the Great Lakes are complex, but historically nesting sites have been lost to development (especially public recreation) as well as other shoreline infrastructure, and possibly to scientific collecting. Since listing, concerns for this population focus on human disturbance from public recreation mortality, and from increases in avian (e.g., crows, ravens, gulls, merlins) and mammalian predators. Ultimate impacts of climate change on plover breeding phenology and habitat are yet to be realized.

Because of the rarity of this species, population trends are monitored closely, especially in the Great Lakes area. Overall, the number of Piping Plovers in North America has increased since all three populations were listed in the mid-1980s, but the population size of the Great Plains birds remains uncertain.

Endangered and Disappearing Birds of the Midwest

Migration routes for the species are known from resightings of color-banded individuals. Birds from the Great Lakes winter on the Atlantic Coast, generally from the Carolinas south to Florida, and then along the Gulf Coast of Florida and west to Texas. A few birds have been observed in the Bahamas, Cuba, and Mexico. Migration routes typically take the birds east to the East Coast and then south, but some plovers travel south via inland routes to their winter sites. Most Great Lakes birds are reported during the winter in South Carolina, Georgia, and Florida, where they inhabit coastal shoreline on the mainland as well as on barrier islands. Unlike other shorebird species, Piping Plovers do not migrate or winter in large concentrations; only one or small numbers are typically reported during the nonbreeding season at any location. Observations of banded birds also reveal that adult pairs do not migrate or winter together, and they are also not seen with their offspring from the previous nesting season. Individuals from the three populations are often reported from the same wintering sites, and this overlap is most pronounced between Great Lakes and Atlantic birds (East Coast) and Great Lakes and Great Plains birds (Gulf Coast).

Identification. During the breeding season, adult Piping Plovers possess *a single black neck band*, a black band across the forehead, and a white line above the eye. The bill is very short and stout, and is *orange with a black tip*. The upper body is pale, the belly white, and the legs orange. In flight a complete white band can be seen across the upper tail feathers, and the tip of the tail is black. Males and females are similar in appearance, but overall the females have less intense coloration.

Vocalizations. Like most birds, Piping Plovers produce a variety of sounds that are associated with specific functions, such as courtship and presence of danger. The most typical vocalization is referred to as the *peep-lo* call, which is given as a contact call between adult plovers or adults and their chicks, particularly as a warning that danger is present.

Nesting. Although not usually considered a "colonial nester," Piping Plovers are attracted to other breeding pairs and often nest in close proximity to each other in the Great Lakes. For example, up to twenty pairs have been recorded on one point on North Manitou Island in the Sleeping Bear Dunes National Lakeshore. In contrast, however, plovers also nest as single pairs at a number of other locations. Suitable habitat includes wide, firm, sandy beaches that are overlaid with a layer of smooth cobble. Vegetation is sparse and nests are often found in association with dunes, river mouths, or points of land that extend out into the water. Plovers typically lay four buff-colored eggs, splotched with black and brown for effective camouflage within their shoreline habitat. Incubation is slightly less than one month (twenty-six to twenty-eight days). Chicks hatch synchronously and leave the nest within less than

a day after hatching. Nests are constructed in cobble and lined with tiny stones. Young feed themselves but depend on adults to brood them during cold or rainy weather, particularly during the first ten days. Both parents care for the young initially, but the adult female typically leaves for fall migration within several weeks after hatching. The male follows once the chicks have fledged. Juveniles are capable of flight after about twenty-three days but often remain in the vicinity of the nest territory for several weeks after the parents have departed.

Francesca Cuthbert

Facing, Piping Plover, April, Texas: Piping Plovers in alternate plumage have pale gray backs, bright-orange legs and feet, an orange bill with a black tip, and a single black band around the neck.

Marbled Godwit
(*Limosa fedoa*)

STATUS:

2014 NABCI Yellow Watch List, 2016 NABCI Watch List, State Species of Special Concern (Minnesota)

ESTIMATED POPULATION TREND:

Recent trends appear stable over the past several decades, but serious declines are thought to have occurred since the late 1800s and early 1900s

LENGTH: 18"

Marbled Godwit, April, Texas: Marbled Godwits have long, distinctive bills that are slightly upturned and bicolored, becoming black at the tip.

Breeding
Migration
Nonbreeding

Species Account. In the late 1800s, the naturalist Thomas Sadler Roberts traveled with a team of scientists through Minnesota gathering information on birds that would become part of the basis for his 1932 work *The Birds of Minnesota*. In reflecting on these travels, Roberts later commented: "The great Marbled Godwit was so abundant, so constant and insistent, in its attentions to the traveler on the prairie, and so noisy that it became at times an actual nuisance. . . . They were continually hovering about the team, perfectly fearless and nearly deafening us with their loud, harsh cries." At one time, Marbled Godwits nested across much of the prairie regions of the Midwest, including portions of Iowa and Wisconsin. There is some evidence that nesting may have occurred at least as far south and east as Indiana. Today, they are gone from these states as a nesting species and only occur sparingly during migration. Even

Facing, Marbled Godwit, February, Florida: Marbled Godwits appear slightly less heavily barred in basic plumage as compared to the breeding season. Godwits use their long bills to probe deep into soft mudflats in search of prey.

in Minnesota, where they were once so abundant, the Marbled Godwit is now a state-designated species of special concern and can be found only at the western edges of the state.

Population trends for the Marbled Godwit are difficult to estimate because the birds' nesting habitat does not match up well with typical routes for the Breeding Bird Survey. Recent estimates, however, place the total world's population of Marbled Godwit at between 140,000 and 200,000 birds. The vast majority of these nest in the prairies and wetlands of the Dakotas, Montana, and south-central Canada, but a few thousand birds nest in two separate populations: one on the rim of James Bay in Canada and one in Alaska. Suitable breeding habitat seems to center on relatively sparse, shortgrass prairie—with the birds often preferring habitat that is being grazed. Ideal habitat includes large blocks of grasslands, as well as a variety of wetland habitats. The draining of wetlands, conversion of prairie for agriculture, and extensive market hunting of godwits in the nineteenth century are all suspected causes of the significant decline in this species's numbers to the low level we see today.

Migration routes for this species are only poorly understood. The majority of the Great Plains population appears to leave the breeding grounds and head south and west to winter on the Pacific Coast of northwestern Mexico, although there is a percentage of this group that is known to winter on the U.S. Gulf Coast. Even less is known of the migration routes of the Alaska and James Bay populations, although it may be that a number of the Marbled Godwits we see during migration around the Great Lakes are birds from the James Bay population. Large concentrations of Marbled Godwits have been recorded at Bear River Migratory Bird Refuge in Utah during migration (more than forty thousand birds), with more birds using this site during fall migration than in the spring. While some birds travel as far south as Latin America, the majority winter in the United States and Mexico. More than half the world population of Marbled Godwits winters on the Pacific Coast between San Francisco Bay and Baja California, with seventy thousand Marbled Godwits found at a single location in Baja California during January 1994—the largest concentration of these birds recorded in recent times.

Identification. The Marbled Godwit is a large shorebird with beautiful, *warm buff tones* marked with darker speckling. The bill is *very long, slightly upturned, and two toned.* The base of the bill is a lighter pink or orange-salmon color that fades to black toward the tip. Birds in flight show cinnamon lining on the wings. Breeding and nonbreeding plumages are similar, but birds show more dark speckling across the breast while in breeding plumage. The Long-billed Curlew is similar in overall size and coloration, but the incredibly long, down-curving bill of the curlew separates this species relatively easily.

Vocalizations. A loud, laughing *radica radica radica* is heard on the breeding grounds. Marbled Godwits are less vocal during migration and winter.

Nesting. Marbled Godwits nest in loose colonies in suitable habitat and lay three to five lightly spotted, olive-colored eggs. Incubation lasts about three weeks, with young leaving the nest shortly after hatching. Nests are placed on the ground in a slight depression lined with dry grasses and sometimes are covered by a partial canopy of grasses arranged over the nest.

Matt Williams

Facing, Marbled Godwit, February, Florida: In flight, Marbled Godwits present a distinctive silhouette and show cinnamon coloration in the wings.

8

Red Knot
(*Calidris canutus*)

STATUS:

2014 NABCI Red Watch List, *C. canutus rufa* subspecies is Federally Threatened. IUCN Near Threatened, State Threatened (Ohio),
State Species of Special Concern (Indiana).

ESTIMATED POPULATION TREND:

Data for this species is not available through the BBS. Estimates
from the major stopover sites suggest a 75 percent population drop
for the subspecies *C. canutus rufa* between 2000 and 2016.

LENGTH: 10.5"

Red Knot, February, Florida: Red Knots have medium-length bills that
are straighter and not as long as those of the Dunlin or dowitchers.

Breeding

Migration

Nonbreeding

Species Account. Perfectly built for long-distance migration, Red Knots are one of the true marvels of the natural world. Weighing less than a cup of coffee, this remarkable bird spends its winters as far south as Tierra del Fuego on the southern tip of South America. As breeding season approaches, the birds migrate north all the way to the Arctic Circle to nest—only to fly back south again after the short breeding season. This amazing journey means that some birds may fly as far as eighteen thousand miles in a single year, and much of that distance is over the open Atlantic Ocean. To fuel their flight, knots are able to pack in incredible amounts of calories during several short stopovers along the way. The birds are faithful to these stopover sites year after year, and in many cases they arrive at the sites emaciated and in need of immediate calories after nonstop flight segments of 1,500 miles or more. At these stopover sites, birds can increase their body weight by as much as 10 percent per day when conditions are good, sometimes doubling their body weight at a stopover site before attempting the next segment of the journey.

One critical stopover site is along the Delaware Bay on the East Coast of the United States. This site is home to the largest concentration of nesting horseshoe crabs in the world, and their eggs make the perfect food for migrating Red Knots. Prior to 1980, numbers of Red Knots using Delaware Bay during the month of May averaged between 100,000 and 150,000 birds. Large-scale commercial harvesting of horseshoe crabs in Delaware Bay began in the 1990s, and today the average number of Red Knots using the area in May is fewer than twenty-six thousand birds. Horseshoe crab harvests are now carefully managed to help stabilize and recover Red Knot populations. In all, there are six subspecies of the Red Knot worldwide—three of which occur in the United States, with *C. canutus rufa* being the one most likely to be seen in the Midwest. It is estimated that as much as 90 percent of the world population of this subspecies of Red Knot can be found on the beaches of Delaware Bay on a single day in May.

Red Knots are somewhat unusual among shorebirds in that for much of the year they eat entire mussels and mollusks—shell and all. However, in preparation for migration, the knot's flight muscles increase in size, but the birds' stomachs and gizzards shrink. With shrunken gizzards, which normally help in digesting food, the birds are forced to search out softer prey during migration, which is part of the reason the soft, nutritious horseshoe crab eggs are so critical for survival. Upon reaching the still-frozen Arctic nesting grounds in June, conditions force the birds either to eat seeds for a short time until insects and invertebrates become available or to survive on the stored fat from their last stopover.

In the Midwest, Red Knots are most commonly spotted along the shores of the Great Lakes. Spring migrants pass through in mid-May to early June. Fall migration is a bit more spread out, with adult birds first appearing in late July to early August. Fall numbers in the Midwest do not reach their peak until September, when juvenile birds pass through.

Identification. Red Knots are the largest of the "peeps" in North America, and are *about the size of a robin*. They are long winged and appear streamlined in flight. In breeding plumage (May-August), they have a *salmon colored breast*, throat and eyeline, with a dappled gray, black, and salmon back. The black bill is relatively short and straight. Nonbreeding plumage (September–April) adults are gray backed with gray chests and barring down the flanks, with a white breast. Juveniles appear similar to nonbreeding adults, but the feathers of the back are edged in white, giving the back a scaly appearance. Nonbreeding plumage birds can be mistaken for the smaller Dunlin, whose beak is longer and droops at the tip.

Vocalizations. Red Knots are usually silent, although they can give a low *wett-wet* call. Males on the breeding grounds give a soft, wailing *quer-wer* call as they fly in high circles over their territory.

Nesting. The nest is a cup-shaped depression on the ground in the open tundra, usually near water. Eggs are faint olive with darker markings concentrated toward the larger end. Young leave the nest shortly after hatching and are tended by both parents for a short time. The female leaves the young to begin her migration southward before the young are able to fly themselves. The first nest of this species was not recorded until 1909 during Admiral Perry's expedition to the North Pole.

Matt Williams

Red Knot, February, Florida: This bird is beginning to transition into alternate plumage. The face and breast are beginning to show some of the salmon-pink coloration of the breeding season.

9

Dunlin
(*Calidris alpina*)

STATUS:

2014 NABCI Yellow Watch List

ESTIMATED POPULATION TREND:

The *C. alpina hudsonia* subspecies that we typically see in the Midwest appears to be stable. However, the *C. alpina arcticola* subspecies that winters in coastal Asia may have declined by as much as 30 percent since 2006.

LENGTH: 8.5"

Dunlin, April, Texas: This Dunlin shows the distinctive long, slightly down-curved bill of the species. In alternate plumage, Dunlins have black bellies and reddish backs.

Breeding
Migration

Species Account. Known as the Grass Snipe to early ornithologists, Pectoral Sandpipers are more likely than many other sandpipers to be found in grassy marshes or flooded fields with vegetation than out in the open on true mudflats—although they can occasionally be found in these habitats as well. While Midwestern birders know the Pectoral Sandpiper quite well as a migrant, the birds' outrageous breeding displays are completely foreign to those who have not traveled to the Arctic tundra. In a 1982 article in *American Birds*, J. P. Myers describes the spectacle of the male Pectoral Sandpiper's hooting displays: "At first hearing one has difficulty accepting its source as avian. The hoot is a fog horn, a sonar beam, an electronic oscillator bearing no relation

to the sounds about it. Even after bird and call are linked it seems preposterous. The way the call is made, the bodily distortions that male goes through to make its hoot, are visually just as odd as is the sound unworldly." An inflatable air sac in the chest allows the birds to create these fantastic noises while doing their flight display, and is also what gives the bird their common name. Typically, the display begins with the male perched on a slight rise on the tundra. He launches into a very low flight just over the female, all the while pumping the balloonlike air sac on his chest and emitting hollow, pulsing hoots. After passing over the female, he turns and flies back to his original perch using a combination of flutters and glides. When the male approaches the female on the ground, he droops his wings and puffs out his chest, showing off the dark bases of his chest feathers. Other calls are given during the display, including a variety of gargling growls. If another male intrudes into his territory, vigorous battles ensue, with feathers occasionally flying during the scuffles.

Pectoral Sandpipers are fairly early spring migrants, with the first birds often spotted in the Midwest in early March. Peak spring numbers are usually reached in April. Occasionally, flocks numbering in the thousands were observed in the Midwest region during the 1970s and 1980s, with a flock of four thousand reported at Newton County, Indiana, on April 3, 1977. Today, spring flocks larger in size than a few hundred birds are unusual. Fall migration begins as early as late June, but more commonly in the first three weeks of July, with the arrival of adult birds. This is followed a few weeks later with an influx of juveniles. Peak numbers in the fall are usually reached in late August and early September, with a few birds sometimes remaining in the area as late as December.

Like most shorebirds, Pectoral Sandpipers undertake amazing migrations. The birds nest across the far reaches of the North American mainland and Arctic islands, and across the Bering Sea in Arctic regions across a good portion of Asia. The majority of the birds migrate to South America for the winter, although small numbers regularly winter in Australia, Tasmania, and New Zealand.

Using surveys of breeding populations in the Arctic, along with estimates of southbound migrants in the Great Plains, a current estimate puts the overall population of Pectoral Sandpipers at 1.6 million birds. It is thought that the population has undergone declines since the 1980s, when numbers were thought to be significantly higher. The U.S. Shorebird Conservation Plan Partnership lists the Pectoral Sandpiper as a species of "high concern" on its 2016 list.

Facing, Pectoral Sandpiper, April, Indiana: The yellow bill and legs, along with the clean line across the breast that separates the streaked chest from the clean, white belly are all helpful field marks.

Identification. The Pectoral Sandpiper is a medium-sized sandpiper with a very slight downward curve to the beak, which is usually lighter at the base than at the tip. *The legs are of medium length and yellowish.* In all plumages, the *breast is darkly streaked and separated from the white underbelly by a crisp, horizontal line.* Males are 10 percent larger than females, but plumages are indistinguishable. Juveniles in the fall have darker feather centers and better-defined white and reddish feather edges, which lends a scaly appearance to the back. The Pectoral Sandpiper looks similar to the Least Sandpiper, but Pectoral Sandpipers are significantly larger, bulkier birds.

Vocalizations. During migration, the vocalizations are largely limited to a reedy *krrrp*. However, on the breeding grounds the male gives a hollow series of hoots and a wide variety of growls and grunts.

Nesting. The nest is a shallow hollow on the ground on grassy tundra. The male may mate with several females. A total of four eggs are typically laid. Eggs are olive with heavy, dark splotches, especially toward the larger end of the egg. The female incubates the eggs and tends the young without help from the male.

Matt Williams

Facing, Pectoral Sandpiper, August, Indiana: As is typical of most shorebirds, fall migration in the Midwest begins with adult Pectoral Sandpipers moving through first, followed by an influx of juveniles that have richer, rustier hues in their plumage than the adults. This bird is an adult.

11

Semipalmated Sandpiper
(*Calidris pusilla*)

STATUS:
2014 NABCI Yellow Watch List, 2016 NABCI Watch List, IUCN Near Threatened

ESTIMATED POPULATION TREND: The population of Semipalmated Sandpipers that breeds in eastern Canada and migrates through the Midwest is thought to have declined by 68%–75% from the 1980s through 2008.

LENGTH: 5–6"

Semipalmated Sandpiper (juvenile), August, Indiana: As is typical of most shorebirds, juveniles show fresh, white feather edges to the upperparts in fall.

Breeding
Migration
Nonbreeding

Species Account. The Semipalmated Sandpiper is a relatively small shorebird that is still fairly common in the Midwest during migration. Breeding near the northern edge of the continent, the birds migrate as far south as South America to reach suitable wintering grounds. Despite weighing only as much as a single slice of bread, at least some Semipalmated Sandpipers may fly nonstop from New England's Atlantic Coast all the way to their wintering grounds—a journey of roughly two thousand miles. To make these long flights, the birds need to have excellent fat reserves. At key stopover sites, Semipalmated Sandpipers will concentrate in large numbers as they feed on high-quality food sources in order to build up reserves as quickly as possible. At peak times, more than three hundred thousand birds may pack into one stopover area if conditions are right. Delaware Bay in New Jersey can see the passage during spring migration of up to 60 percent of the entire population of these birds, which time

their arrival to feast on horseshoe crab eggs in late May. Ensuring that the birds have access to excellent food sources at these stopovers at the right time of year becomes critical to preserving Semipalmated Sandpipers, as well as many other shorebird species.

Semipalmated Sandpipers get their name because of the partial webbing between the toes of their feet, although this is very hard to see unless the bird is in one's hand. The only other small sandpiper to share this trait is the Western Sandpiper. This webbing may help the birds as they forage in a variety of shallow-water habitats, including intertidal mudflats, shallow estuaries, and inland marshes.

Semipalmated Sandpipers feed largely on a variety of small aquatic and terrestrial invertebrates. During breeding season their diet consists primarily of insects, especially flies and their larvae,

Semipalmated Sandpiper, May, Indiana: In flight, Semipalmated Sandpipers show a thin white line that runs most of the length of the wing.

as well as spiders, snails, and some seeds. During migration and on the wintering grounds, the birds feed on a wide variety of small crustaceans that live in shallow water or wet mud, as well as many insects, small mollusks, and worms.

Although Breeding Bird Survey data do not exist for this or most other Arctic breeding species, there have been efforts undertaken to census the population of this species during migration and on the wintering grounds—as well as recent efforts to survey the breeding population in portions of the Arctic. Surveys done from the air along the wintering grounds in northern South America—along the coasts of Suriname, French Guiana, and Guyana—suggest that the nonbreeding population using these areas may have declined by more than 75 percent between the early 1980s and 2008. Counts done on the Bay of Fundy during fall migration indicate a drop of 68 percent during a similar time period. It is thought that overharvesting of horseshoe crabs in the United States before new restrictions went into place, especially during the late 1990s, may have contributed significantly to these declines. In addition, legal and illegal shooting of Semipalmated Sandpipers in South America is estimated to result in the mortality of roughly twenty thousand birds per year. Although the population of Semipalmated Sandpipers breeding in eastern Canada seems to have significantly

Endangered and Disappearing Birds of the Midwest

Semipalmated Sandpiper, May, Indiana: In alternate
plumage, Semipalmated Sandpipers show a black
beak, black or gray legs, a brownish back, and a
white breast with light streaking on the chest.

declined, the breeding populations in northwest Canada and Alaska appear to be
holding relatively stable, and the overall total population may still number more than
two million birds.

Identification. Semipalmated Sandpipers are small shorebirds with *neat, fine streaking on the chest and pure white underparts.* Their backs are mottled with black, gray, and brown. The bill is black and relatively short, and appears rounded at the tip. *Legs are black or gray.* During breeding season the cheek and cap can appear more reddish brown. Juveniles appear to have more reddish tones and more defined scalloping on the back. In flight, the tail has a black central line with white marks on either side and a thin white line on the wings. The Least Sandpiper is similar looking but has yellowish legs instead of dark legs, and it is slightly smaller.

Vocalizations. The call is a rapid, liquid chattering primarily on one pitch. This is sometimes given in flight during territorial displays on the breeding grounds.

Nesting. Three to four off-white eggs blotched with brown and gray are incubated by both parents. Young leave the nest within hours of hatching. The male will make multiple scrapes for a nest, and the female will choose one and add nesting material to the site, including grasses and moss.

Matt Williams

12 American Woodcock
(*Scolopax minor*)

STATUS:
   2014 NABCI Yellow Watch List, 2016 NABCI Watch List

ESTIMATED POPULATION TREND:
   >−40% since 1966

LENGTH: 10–12"

Breeding
Nonbreeding
Year-round

Species Account. Bog sucker, mud bat, timberdoodle—for one bird to be known by these descriptive, although not necessarily complimentary names, it must be a truly unusual species. Unusual certainly describes the American Woodcock. Technically a shorebird, the American Woodcock makes its home in young forest stands instead of beaches and mudflats. Wintering across the southeastern United States, Woodcocks return to the Midwest as early as February. The males establish singing grounds at forest clearings, old fields, or other openings, and give a nasal peent call from the ground. After calling, the male will launch into the air, wings twittering, and quickly gain altitude until it reaches a height of between 200 and 350 feet. While circling high overhead as part of the elaborate "sky dance," the male gives a rapid, high-pitched series

Facing, American Woodcock, May, Ohio: The American Woodcock prefers damp woodlands, where it can easily probe its long beak into the ground in search of earthworms.

of chirps that rhythmically rise and fall in pitch before he plunges back to the earth, flaring at the last moment to safely arrive at the same point he departed from. Male American Woodcocks may use multiple singing grounds, and females often visit four or more of these display grounds before nesting. The woodcock is the earliest nesting ground bird in the country, as it often lays eggs in March.

Up to 75 percent of the diet of the American Woodcock is made up of earthworms. Other prey items include spiders, snails, millipedes, and ants, along with a small amount of plant material. The Woodcock uses its long bill to probe deeply into soft, moist earth in search of prey. The tip of the bill can be opened and closed even while underground, and both the bill and tongue are rough, to aid in the capture of slippery prey. Occasionally Woodcocks perish after arriving on the breeding grounds when a late period of extended freezing weather makes their prey inaccessible.

The American Woodcock Conservation Plan used Singing Ground Survey results to estimate the population change from the 1970s levels through the early 2000s. The results showed a decline from 3,073,339 displaying males down to 2,244,008 (27% decline) displaying males over the roughly thirty-year period. Breeding Bird Survey data indicate a decline of more than 40 percent continent-wide since 1966. In some Midwestern states, the losses may be even more severe, with BBS data indicating declines of more than 80 percent in Minnesota and Indiana. Loss of habitat is thought to be the primary reason for the declines. Historically, fire would have played a major role in maintaining early successional forested habitat. With more effective fire suppression and changes in forest management practices, more Midwestern forested acres are ending up in an older-age class that is not suitable for woodcocks or other declining birds that need some form of regular disturbance, which maintains young forest or other early successional habitats. It is estimated that to return to 1970s levels of American Woodcocks, we need to add twenty million acres of early successional, brushy forest habitat in the United States, primarily in the Midwest and Northeast.

Identification. The American Woodcock is a *stocky, short-legged bird* of shrubby young forest, old fields, brushy swamps, thickets along streams, and other forest edges and openings. American Woodcocks have a long pink bill, a rusty tail, and mottling with brown, gray, and black. The belly is a warm, buffy color. They have a strongly patterned head, with *three chocolate-colored bars separated by thin, buff-colored stripes.* Their large, dark eyes are far back on their heads, allowing for sight in all directions even while feeding. The Common Snipe is similar in size and body shape but lacks the buffy tones of the Woodcock.

Vocalizations. On the ground, the woodcock gives a loud, buzzy *peent* call that is somewhat similar to that of the Common Nighthawk. In the air, the wings make a whistling noise.

Nesting. Nests are on the ground, usually in a shallow depression 5 inches across and 1.5 inches deep. Typically, four rosy eggs splotched with brown are laid. The female may abandon the nest if disturbed early on. Later during incubation, she may give a distraction display if approached, feigning injury to lure a predator from the nest. Young leave the nest almost immediately after hatching and can start to catch their own food within a few days. Young birds become independent within about a month.

Matt Williams

13 Lesser Yellowlegs
(*Tringa flavipes*)

STATUS:

2014 NABCI Yellow Watch List, 2016 NABCI Watch List

ESTIMATED POPULATION TREND:

Some surveys of portions of the South American coastline show an 80% decline in wintering Lesser Yellowlegs, although it is difficult to say whether that is representative of their range-wide population trends.

LENGTH: 10.5"

Breeding

Migration

Nonbreeding

Species Account. The Lesser Yellowlegs is a fairly common spring and fall migrant across much of the Midwest. It can often be found with the slightly larger Greater Yellowlegs at wetlands, in flooded agricultural fields, and along shorelines. Lesser Yellowlegs pursue prey of many kinds, including small fish and crustaceans. They seem to favor aquatic insects, however, and much of their summer diet is made up of beetles, water boatmen, and different life stages of other insects such as crane flies and dragonflies. In the Midwest, spring passage is largely in the month of April, with fall migrants showing up as early as July. Within our region, Union Slough National Wildlife Refuge in Iowa may have the highest concentrations of birds, with as many as six thousand being reported at one time.

Facing, Lesser Yellowlegs, April, Indiana: Lesser Yellowlegs can be found in the spring across the Midwest in wetlands, along shorelines, and in small puddles in agricultural fields. The long, yellow legs are distinctive even at a distance, and the shorter, smaller bill separates this species from the similar Greater Yellowlegs.

In the late 1800s, the Lesser Yellowlegs likely suffered significant population declines because of widespread sport and market hunting of this and other shorebird species. Although it is difficult to put a number on the total population of that time, or how much it declined, hunters of the era reported taking more than twenty birds with a single shot because of the densities of the flocks. After the Migratory Bird Treaty Act was passed in 1918, hunting pressure on shorebirds in the United States declined. However, Lesser Yellowlegs and other shorebirds are still hunted in portions of their winter range. For example, in Barbados there are artificially maintained wetlands known as shooting swamps that are managed for hunting shorebirds. In fact, the last known Eskimo Curlew to be killed by hunters was at a shooting swamp in Barbados. Tens of thousands of shorebirds are thought to be taken here each year. Estimates are that Lesser Yellowlegs make up between 40 percent and 60 percent of the total birds shot. Recently, some shooting swamps have begun to limit shooting of certain declining species, and others are working to implement sustainable harvest quotas that will allow for hunters to continue to maintain the habitat for the birds, but with more protections in place to limit their harvests.

As hunting in the Caribbean and in South America becomes better managed, it is likely that hunting will have only minor impacts on yellowlegs populations. However, other threats to the birds remain. Habitat loss is likely the most serious threat, with nesting habitat in the boreal forest being lost to energy development, and wetlands being converted in the wintering range to agricultural use.

It is still difficult today to get firm numbers on the overall population size, or population trends for the Lesser Yellowlegs. Data from the Breeding Bird Survey indicate an overall decline of more than 90 percent since 1966, although the survey's routes primarily cover the southern edges of the birds' breeding range and may not accurately reflect population trends across the entire breeding range. Other studies have attempted to look at the numbers of Lesser Yellowlegs found at migratory stopover sites and at their wintering grounds in order to understand population trends. In Ontario, Canada, the numbers of both Greater and Lesser Yellowlegs recorded at stopover sites declined by an average of 4.9 percent per year from 1974 to 1989. The decline was even more rapid from 1989 to 2009, with an average decline of over 11 percent per year. On the wintering grounds along the coast of Suriname in South America, aerial surveys, accompanied by ground-based observations, reveal the Lesser Yellowlegs population wintering there may have declined by more than 80 percent between 2002 and 2009. The best current estimate puts the total population of Lesser Yellowlegs at 660,000 birds, although other estimates have ranged from 300,000 to 400,000.

Lesser Yellowlegs, April, Indiana: Alternate-plumage birds like the one pictured here are darker and more heavily marked than birds with basic plumage, which appear more uniformly light gray.

Identification. The Lesser Yellowlegs is a medium-sized shorebird with long, bright-yellow legs. The back is a mottled brown, and the underparts are white, with brown speckles across the chest. In flight, a white rump patch is visible. The Greater Yellowlegs is very similar in appearance, but when seen side by side, the Greater Yellowlegs is larger and has a longer, heavier bill that is often bicolored and may appear to be slightly upturned.

Vocalizations. Call is a piping *tu-tu* given in flight or when perched. The call is a useful way to differentiate the Lesser from the Greater Yellowlegs, as the Greater's typical call consists of three notes instead of the two-note call of the Lesser Yellowlegs.

Nesting. Lesser Yellowlegs nest in open boreal forest (sometimes in burned areas) with scattered wetlands. The nest is a depression on the ground or in moss, sometimes near the base of a bush. The nest can be lined with grasses, leaves, or spruce needles. The clutch consists of three to four buff eggs blotched with brown. The female often departs before the chicks can fly, leaving the male to defend the young.

Matt Williams

Facing, Greater Yellowlegs (for comparison), January, Louisiana: This Greater Yellowlegs looks very similar to a basic-plumage Lesser Yellowlegs. However, the Greater Yellowlegs is taller and heavier bodied, and the bill is longer and heavier with a slight two-toned appearance that grows darker toward the tip.

14 Willet
(*Tringa semipalmata*)

STATUS:

2014 NABCI Yellow Watch List, 2016 NABCI Watch List

ESTIMATED POPULATION TREND:

BBS data would indicate a drop of roughly 18% since 1966, although other sources show a stable population during the same period.

LENGTH: 15"

Willet, April, Texas: The Willet has a long, straight bill and thick gray legs that help distinguish it from other large shorebirds.

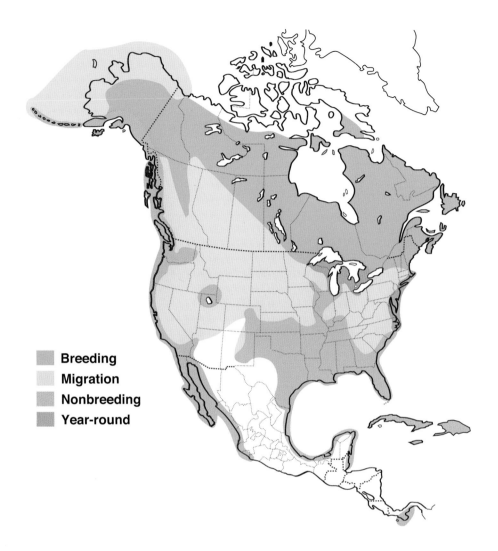

Breeding
Migration
Nonbreeding
Year-round

Species Account. The Herring Gull is a large, familiar gull that is often seen along the Great Lakes, inland lakes, and even plowed fields, parking lots, garbage dumps, airports, and other open areas. Herring Gulls are quite variable in appearance. Nine different subspecies are recognized, and hybridization regularly occurs with other large gulls like the Glaucous-winged Gull and the Lesser Black-backed Gull. In addition, Herring Gulls change substantially in appearance as they age. First-year birds are quite dark overall but become lighter each year as they age, taking four years to develop full adult plumage. The pink legs and overall large size of the birds are constant in all plumages and may be some of the better field marks.

Herring Gulls feed on a wide assortment of prey. They are opportunistic and will feed on carcasses or steal prey from other birds. Fish, crabs, mussels, crayfish, worms, other birds, and even garbage are all common food items. Some males have even been

Herring Gull, January, Louisiana: This adult Herring Gull
in flight shows the black wing tips with the white
"windows" on the outer primary feathers.

Endangered and Disappearing Birds of the Midwest

reported to feed on chicks from other Herring Gull nests. Herring Gulls have been observed taking flight with hard-shelled prey items and carrying them above rocks to drop them from a higher altitude, apparently to crack the shells and make it easier to access the meat. Others have reported seeing the closely related European Herring Gull use bread as bait to attract fish, which are then captured when they rise to the surface to feed on the bread. A study of Herring Gulls during winter on the Great Lakes found that the most common prey fish included rainbow smelt, alewife, and freshwater drum. Garbage was also a significant part of the winter diet, as were small

Herring Gull, January, Louisiana: This basic-plumage Herring Gull shows darker streaking around the head, which would be pure white in alternate plumage.

Herring Gull, June, Michigan: This adult Herring Gull is in alternate plumage, showing an all-white head with a red spot on the lower mandible of the bill and pink legs.

mammals such as deer mice. Over the open ocean, Herring Gulls will follow ships or whales to snatch prey that comes to the surface from the disturbance. They are capable of drinking saltwater from the ocean because of their special glands that excrete salt, which would otherwise dehydrate them.

Because they are predators, pollutants such as PCBs (polychlorinated biphenyls, which are man-made organic chemicals) and metals accumulate in Herring Gulls making them a "sentinel species" that may provide us with early warnings about overall environmental health. Studies by the Canadian Wildlife Service and the Michigan Department of Environmental Quality have used the eggs of Herring Gulls for decades

Endangered and Disappearing Birds of the Midwest

as a way to track the level of pollutants in the Great Lakes. The most recent results show an increase in several relatively new and poorly understood substances that are toxic to wildlife and are accumulating in the Great Lakes. This new class of pollutants includes flame-retardant chemicals, adhesives, stain repellants, and lubricants. Little is known about these chemicals, but further Herring Gull research may help to identify how these pollutants could affect the health of birds and other life.

It appears that while Herring Gulls are being pushed out of the far northern reaches of their breeding range by the larger Great Black-backed Gull, they are successfully expanding their range to the south along the Atlantic Coast. Despite this range expansion, the overall population has decreased by 83 percent between 1966 and 2015. Although there still may be nearly a quarter million birds, it is thought that the numbers have declined so steeply for several reasons. Overfishing, changes in fishing practices, human disturbance of nesting sites, and pollution are all potential causes of the decline.

Identification. Juvenile birds are all *chocolate brown with a black bill*. As they age, they become more mottled gray and white. In their fourth winter, they reach adult plumage. Adults during the breeding season have all-white heads and bellies, white tails, gray backs, and black wing tips. The beak is *yellow orange with a circular reddish spot* on the lower mandible toward the tip. Feet are pinkish in all plumages. Adults in winter have heavy streaking on the head. The Glaucous-winged Gull is similar but has white wing tips, unlike the black of the Herring Gull.

Vocalizations. Herring gulls make a variety of calls, including a repeated loud, laughing *kuk-kuk-kuk* and a short four-part *ha-ha-ha-ha* alarm call, a plaintive higher-pitched yeow, and a variety of other loud cries.

Nesting. One to three buff or olive eggs are laid in May. They are typically heavily marked with darker brown. Both the male and female incubate the eggs. Upon hatching, young are fed day and night for up to twelve weeks by the adults who regurgitate prey items at the nest to feed the chicks. Chicks may be fed as much as half a pound of food per day.

Matt Williams

16 Snowy Owl
(*Bubo scandiacus*)

STATUS:
 2014 NABCI Yellow Watch List, 2016 NABCI Watch
 List, 2016 PIF Watch List

ESTIMATED POPULATION TREND:
 –64% during the period 1970–2014

LENGTH: 24"

Breeding
Nonbreeding
Year-round
Irruptive

Species Account. Weighing in at anywhere from four to six pounds, the Snowy Owl is the heaviest owl in North America—about twice as heavy as the taller Great Gray Owl. It is thought that Snowy Owls are heavier than other similarly sized birds because of their dense feathers that are helpful for better insulation and to trap body heat. The extra warmth must come in handy for a bird that nests in the harsh environments of the Arctic.

Interestingly, Snowy Owls appear to only breed during times when high-quality prey is available at a certain density. Evidence suggests that the owls will travel great distances looking for a suitable nesting site where prey densities are high. During the

Facing, Snowy Owl, January, Michigan: Snowy Owls generally show fewer dark markings as they age, with males having fewer markings than females. This bird is likely an adult female or a young male.

breeding season, the birds key in on small mammals—specifically lemmings and voles. Studies from Greenland have shown that unless the density of lemmings is near a minimum of one per acre or greater at the time of snowmelt, the birds will not attempt to nest. In addition, the prey items' average weight must be more than 1.2 ounces in order to entice the birds to attempt to nest. Other research indicates that clutch size can also be affected by prey weight, with larger clutches of owl eggs being laid in years when average prey weight was at least 2.1 ounces.

Because of the variability of prey populations, local numbers of Snowy Owls can be dramatically different from one year to the next. For example, on Banks Island in the Canadian Arctic, the population of Snowy Owls has ranged from two thousand birds to twenty thousand. The birds nesting locations in remote areas of the Arctic also makes estimating population size difficult. Partners in Flight estimates the global population to be two hundred thousand birds, but the Snowy Owl Working Group puts the total population at only thirty thousand pairs.

In the Midwest, the Snowy Owl is seen only in the winter. Even then, the likelihood of seeing these majestic white hunters of the north varies greatly from year to year. In some winters, there are only a handful of birds that winter in our region. In other winters, birds may come much farther south than normal and be present in tremendous numbers. In some years, more than twenty different owls can be seen in a morning by driving the back roads around Snowy Owl hot spots, like Rudyard township in the Upper Peninsula of Michigan. These winters are referred to as "invasion" years. The winter of 2013–2014 was one of the largest invasion years on record. Snowy Owls were reported from across the Midwest in great numbers, and even occurred as far south as Florida and Bermuda.

Until recently, it was thought that these invasions were the result of crashes in the numbers of the birds' prey items in the Arctic, resulting in starving birds traveling south in search of food. However, researchers captured and weighed Snowy Owls during the 2013 invasion and found that the vast majority of birds had healthy body weights and good amounts of fat stores. Using GPS trackers, researchers also found that most of the birds were successfully returning to the Arctic the following spring. All this would appear to indicate that the invasion years are caused when prey availability is high in the Arctic, which results in high breeding success for the owls, apparently causing large numbers to move south in search of suitable wintering grounds.

Identification. Snowy Owls are *large, mostly white owls* that are more active than other owls during daylight hours. They are typically found in open country, which can include beaches, agricultural fields, airports, and tundra. Young birds and females tend to have more of the chocolate chevron or barring pattern than males. All birds become less heavily barred as they age, and older males can be almost pure white. The

Snowy Owl, January, Michigan: Because of the mostly white plumage with few markings, this bird is probably a male.

large, bright yellow eyes also help distinguish this species from the Barn Owl, which can also appear to be mostly white in color.

Vocalizations. Snowy Owls are mostly silent away from the breeding grounds. Birds have been reported, though, to give hoarse croaks and sharp whistles.

Nesting. A ridge or slight rise in the open tundra is often chosen as a nest site. The birds nest in a shallow depression on the ground, and the female will typically lay between three and eleven eggs, with the number depending on available prey. Prey items for nestlings are primarily small mammals like lemmings and voles, but Purple Sandpiper, Rock Ptarmigan, and Snow Bunting remains have also been found in nests. Other prey includes arctic fox, rabbits, and sea ducks.

Matt Williams

17 Short-eared Owl
(*Asio flammeus*)

STATUS:

Common Bird in Steep Decline, State Special Concern (Minnesota),
State Endangered (Illinois, Indiana, Iowa, Michigan)

ESTIMATED POPULATION TREND:

Precise population trends are difficult to establish because of the
nomadic nature of this species. Declines are suspected in at least
certain geographies within the overall range, including the Midwest.

LENGTH: 16"

Breeding

Nonbreeding

Year-round

Species Account. Flying more like a huge butterfly than a bird, Short-eared Owls prefer the open habitats of grasslands and marshes. They fly low and buoyantly over the grasses, slowly flapping their wings, twisting and wheeling back over an area, or hovering in place to further investigate any sounds or movements. The true ears of these birds are small openings on either side of the head that are positioned at slightly different heights to allow them to pinpoint the exact location of any sound. In addition to their sense of hearing, they also hunt visually, quickly dropping to the ground to grab their prey.

Short-eared Owls' main prey items are small mammals, especially voles, mice, shrews, and gophers. Especially in coastal areas, they also take birds, which they often consume only after first removing the wings. Small birds are consumed whole once

Facing, Short-eared Owl, January, Indiana: Even when seen up close, the "ears" are often hard to see, giving Short-eared Owls a smooth-headed appearance.

the wings are removed, but the owls primarily consume only the breast meat of larger birds after decapitating them. While their favorite prey is small mammals, Short-eared Owls will kill mammals as large as rabbits and muskrats. Moles, weasels, and bats are occasionally taken as well.

It is possible to see these birds during the day, especially when it is overcast. However, it is more common for them to roost during daylight hours and be more visible at dawn and dusk. During the winter, Short-eared Owls form communal roosts in areas with high prey densities. These roosts are usually on the ground and may hold as many as two hundred birds. The birds often occupy the same habitat as Northern Harriers. In the evening, about an hour or two before sunset, it is sometimes possible to observe interactions between the two species.

Across a portion of the Midwest, Short-eared Owls are seen only during the winter months, but from Iowa to northern Illinois and Indiana northward, breeding does occur. One of the few owls to make its own nest, Short-eared Owls construct a depression on the ground that is usually concealed in grasses and sometimes lined with feathers. The female can lay as many as eleven eggs in a single clutch, although four to seven is more typical. Under favorable conditions, Short-eared Owls may attempt two broods per year.

Identification. Short-eared Owls are medium-sized owls of open country. Males and females are similar, with the female averaging slightly darker than the male. They have *dark, comma-shaped marks at the bend in the underside of their wings*, and dark vertical streaking on an otherwise buff-colored belly. The upper wing shows a pale crescent in the primaries. Bright-yellow eyes are set in black circles, giving them the appearance of having a black eye. They have *buoyant, butterfly-like flight* as they cruise low over the vegetation searching for a meal. As the name suggests, these birds do have small "ear" tufts on their head, which are often impossible to see in the field. Similar species include Northern Harrier and Long-eared Owl. The former has a much longer tail and usually stops hunting about the time of day the Short-eared Owls emerge, whereas the latter prefers woodland habitats instead of open lands.

Vocalizations. Short-eared Owls give a variety of calls, including hoots and odd, barking calls that sound like a dog. These sounds can be made from the ground or from a perch, or given in flight. Short-eared Owls will also make a clapping or slapping noise with their wings during display flights in the breeding season.

Facing, Short-eared Owl, January, Indiana: In flight, Short-eared Owls have a dark, comma-shaped mark visible on the underside of the bend of the wings.

Endangered and Disappearing Birds of the Midwest

Short-eared Owl, January, Indiana: Dark patches around the eyes give Short-eared Owls the appearance of being masked.

Nesting. Short-eared Owls have nested at least in small numbers in every state in the Midwest. Today, only a handful can be found during the breeding season in the more southern states in the region, with numbers increasing as one moves north into Michigan, Wisconsin, and Minnesota. Nests are constructed on the ground solely by the female, who often chooses a location on a small hummock or rise, or occasionally under a small shrub. She lays anywhere from three to eleven eggs, but six to eight is most typical. Incubation lasts between twenty-four and thirty-seven days, and the male brings food to the female during this time. The young are capable of flight between twenty-seven and thirty-six days but may leave the nest on foot before that.

Matt Williams

Above, Short-eared Owl, January, Indiana: Short-eared Owls are more commonly active during daylight hours than most other North American owl species. It is not unusual to see these birds hunting in the late afternoon, especially on cloudy days.

18 Red-headed Woodpecker
(*Melanerpes erythrocephalus*)

STATUS:
2014 NABCI Yellow Watch List,
2016 NABCI Watch List, 2016 PIF Watch List

ESTIMATED POPULATION TREND:
−68% during the period 1970–2014

LENGTH: 10"

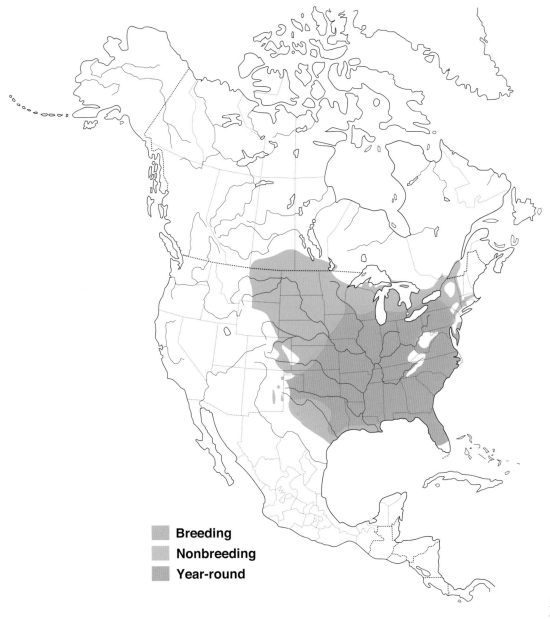

Breeding

Nonbreeding

Year-round

Species Account. Red-headed Woodpeckers are beautiful, noisy, eye-catching birds. Perhaps for these reasons, they have sparked the interest of many young birdwatchers, drawing them into a lifelong pursuit, including the famous ornithologist Alexander Wilson. The Red-headed Woodpecker has been called by many colorful nicknames over the years as well, including shirttail bird, flag bird, and the flying checkerboard. The bird was also used as a symbol of war by Native Americans, with the bloodred heads of these woodpeckers used by Plains tribes as battle ornaments.

Facing, Red-headed Woodpecker, April, Indiana: Red-headed Woodpeckers prefer open canopied forest with many snags where they can perch, then fly out and catch insects on the wing.

Red-headed Woodpecker, April, Indiana: The only woodpecker in the Midwest with a completely red head, adult birds of this species are unmistakable. Young birds look similar to adults but have a brownish-gray head instead of brilliant red.

Red-headed Woodpeckers are unusual birds. They are one of only a handful of woodpecker species that cache their food. They wedge acorns, seeds, and even large insects into nooks and crannies in trees to be eaten at a later date. They are also more adept at catching insects on the wing than any other woodpecker in the Midwest. They can be seen in open forest or clearings, flying out from a tree and snatching a bug before returning to their perch. Perhaps it is this habit that makes them prefer more open forest or savanna habitats rather than heavily wooded tracts.

Red-headed Woodpeckers are omnivorous and have a more varied diet than other woodpeckers. The birds' diet shifts seasonally, but overall it consists of approximately one-third animal material (largely insects like cicadas, beetles, grasshoppers, and

Endangered and Disappearing Birds of the Midwest

bees) and two-thirds plant material, such as acorns, beechnuts, and fruit. Red-headed Woodpeckers will occasionally be seen hopping on the ground looking for food, and they also eat earthworms and, rarely, small rodents. They have even been reported to occasionally take other birds' eggs or nestlings as prey.

In the northern portions of the Midwest, Red-headed Woodpeckers are present during the breeding season but migrate south to warmer climates for the winter. However, across a good portion of the Midwest, they are present year-round in suitable habitat. In addition to north-south migration, the Red-headed Woodpecker also moves somewhat nomadically east and west. These movements may be in response to food availability, as nut (mast) production can vary widely across the birds' range.

There are likely several reasons for the decline of the Red-headed Woodpecker, including collisions with vehicles and competition with other species for cavity nest sites. Wildfires used to play a role in maintaining the more open forest that the birds need, as well as providing large numbers of dead standing trees for nesting. Selective thinning in woods and prescribed burning may improve habitat for the Red-headed Woodpecker by thinning the understory and creating dead snags for roosting and nesting.

Identification. The belly of the Red-headed Woodpecker is snow white, and the beak and feet are a bluish gray. In the Midwest, no other bird has the combination of a completely red head with black wings with white wing patches. The Red-bellied Woodpecker is similar in size but has red only on the back of its head. The Pileated Woodpecker also has black-and-white wings with a red crest on its head but is much larger than the Red-headed Woodpecker. Male and female plumages are identical. Juveniles' appearance is similar to that of adults, but they have a brownish head instead of a bright-red one.

Vocalizations. A sharp, raspy *cheer* is the most commonly heard call. Sometimes the birds give a lower, more rolling chur call that is repeated more rapidly. Red-headed Woodpeckers also drum on trees, branches, and occasionally houses.

Nesting. Red-headed Woodpeckers can create a cavity suitable for nesting in about two weeks. The male does the majority of the excavation and usually chooses a dead or decaying tree or branch. The cavity can be more than a foot deep, with an entrance hole about two inches in diameter. Nest sites are often used again the following year, and they can benefit other species of wildlife that use cavities but are not able to create them. The female lays between three and ten pure-white eggs that take about two weeks to hatch.

Matt Williams

Red-headed Woodpecker, April, Indiana:
In flight, Red-headed Woodpeckers reveal
striking contrasts between the black of the
back and their large white wing patches.

19 Loggerhead Shrike
(*Lanius ludovicianus*)

STATUS:

Common Bird in Steep Decline, L. ludovicianus mearnsi subspecies listed as federally Endangered, State Threatened in Illinois and Minnesota, State Endangered in Indiana, Michigan, Ohio, and Wisconsin

ESTIMATED POPULATION TREND:

−76% during the period 1966–2015

LENGTH: 8–10"

Horned Lark, December, Indiana: The female
Horned Lark has a facial pattern that is not as bold as
that of the male, with less black around the eyes.

Vocalizations. Song is high pitched and often given in flight, sometimes at great height. It consists of several introductory notes followed by a tinkling warble that rises in pitch. Call is a high and weak *see-tu*.

Nesting. Nests are small scrapes on the ground in open country. There is a cup of stems, grass, and other plant material loosely woven together. Between two and seven eggs are laid, with a typical clutch size of four gray eggs with heavy reddish speckles. Young are fed by both parents, and leave the nest at nine to twelve days of age.

Matt Williams

Bank Swallow
(*Riparia riparia*)

STATUS:
   Common Bird in Steep Decline

ESTIMATED POPULATION TREND:
   –94% during the period 1966–2014

LENGTH: 5″

Bank Swallow, May, Indiana: The Bank Swallow is the smallest swallow in the United States and looks similar to the Northern Rough-winged Swallow, except that the Bank Swallow has a brown band across the chest.

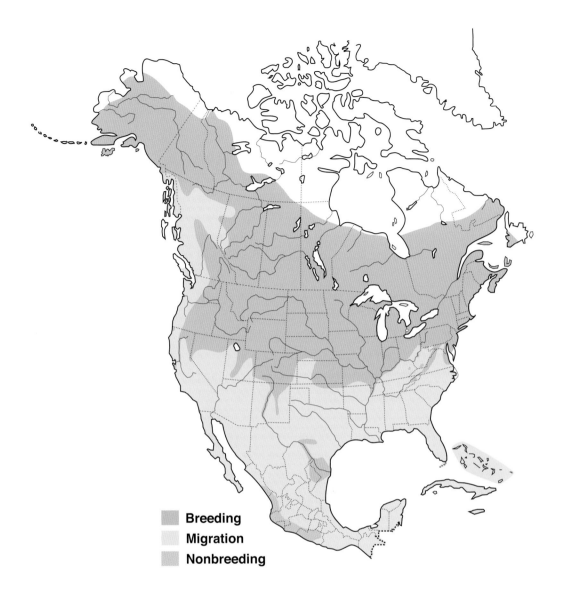

Breeding
Migration
Nonbreeding

Species Account. The Bank Swallow is a very widespread bird. In North America, the birds nest across the northern half of the lower forty-eight states, as well as most of Canada and Alaska. While some birds winter along the Pacific Coast of Mexico, the bulk of the population winters in South America, with especially large numbers in Suriname and Brazil. Some birds travel as far south as the southern tip of the South American mainland. The Bank Swallow can also be found in Europe and Africa, although there it is called the Sand Martin.

Historically, the Bank Swallow nested primarily along riverbanks and other naturally occurring steep slopes where the birds could excavate their nesting burrows in the side of the bank and be relatively free from the threat of predators. Although the birds still use these habitats, many large nesting colonies today are found in gravel pits or in the steep banks where roads were cut through the sides of hills. Colonies of Bank Swallows can be very busy places, with anywhere from ten to a few hundred or more

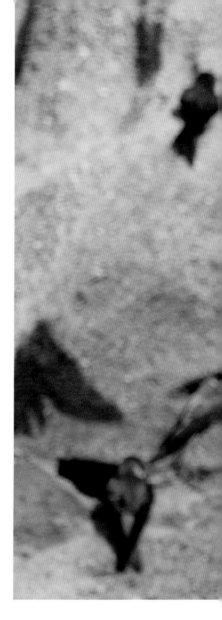

burrows in a single colony. A few colonies may contain as many as two thousand burrows, although about 50 percent of all burrows in Bank Swallow colonies are typically unoccupied. Males use their beaks, wings, and feet to excavate the burrows, which can extend two feet or more into the earth. The females fly through the colony and hover in front of burrow entrances to choose a mate. Once the female chooses a burrow, she may do some additional digging herself, and she completes the actual nest structure by bringing in grasses, small roots, and leaves to form a mat at the end of the burrow.

Bank Swallows feed almost exclusively on insects that they snatch from the air while on the wing. Prey items include ants, flies, bees, beetles, dragonflies, moths, and butterflies. The birds typically forage over lakes, streams, rivers, and open pastures, but they are occasionally seen in feeding flights over wooded areas. During the nesting season, most feeding takes place within about 650 feet from the nesting colony. The birds drink by swooping low over a water body and scooping up water using their lower mandible.

Although Bank Swallows are widespread and still estimated to number 19 million worldwide, the numbers in North America appear to be dropping dramatically. Breeding Bird Survey data indicate a drop of more than 90 percent since 1966. However, because these birds are concentrated near the colony, and because colony sites are frequently abandoned or moved because of changing conditions, it is likely that BBS data is not the best way to estimate population trends for this species.

With recent data coming to light regarding rapidly declining insect populations in the United States, Europe, and other places, it does seem logical that a bird like the Bank Swallow that feeds almost exclusively on airborne insects would be in decline, along with its prey populations. Neonicotinoids and other pesticides are often cited as one potential cause for the declines in honey bees, monarch butterflies, and legions of other less-high-profile insect species. A recent study from Germany documents an 80 percent decline in insect biomass over the past few decades. Many of the chemical components of neonicotinoids have been banned in much of Europe because of concerns about their unintended impacts on nontarget insect species and other life.

Identification. Males and females are impossible to separate in the field. Bank Swallows have *brown backs and white underparts, with a brown band across the upper chest* that separates the white throat from the white belly. Northern Rough-winged Swallows are similar in appearance but lack the brown chest band and have light-brown throats.

Vocalizations. A short, burry *trit-trit*, or harsh chattering.

Nesting. Bank Swallows typically lay four to five white eggs. Incubation and feeding duties are performed by both parents. The young birds will fledge from the nest within about three weeks of hatching.

Matt Williams

22 Wood Thrush
(*Hylocichla mustelina*)

STATUS:

2014 NABCI Yellow Watch List, 2016 NABCI
Watch List, 2016 PIF Watch List

ESTIMATED POPULATION TREND:

−62% during the period 1966–2015

LENGTH: 8"

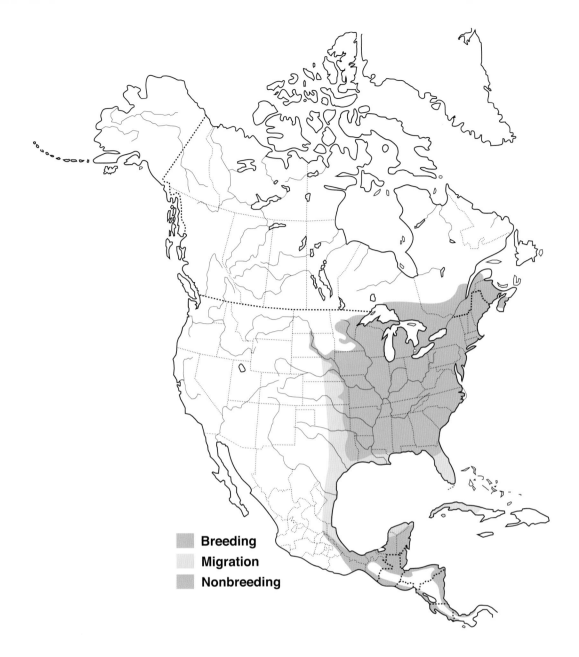

Breeding
Migration
Nonbreeding

Species Account. The enchanting song of the Wood Thrush can be heard drifting from within shaded woodlands in the Midwest and much of the Eastern United States. Because of a dual-chambered voice box, the Wood Thrush can make its own harmonies by singing two different notes at the same time. The result is a melancholy, chorded, flutelike song that has captured many with its beauty. In his journal, Henry David Thoreau wrote of the Wood Thrush: "This is the only bird whose note affects me like music. It lifts and exhilarates me. It is inspiring. It changes all hours to an eternal morning."

The song of the Wood Thrush has three separate parts. Part A consists of several short introductory notes, part B is the familiar *ee-oo-lay*, and part C consists of pairs of notes sung at the same time, which creates a chorded sound. Male Wood Thrushes

Facing, Wood Thrush, May, Indiana: Wood Thrushes have large, rounded black spots on the chest that extend further down the belly than other thrushes in the Midwest.

Wood Thrush, May, Ohio: Although Wood Thrushes usually sing from a perch, they will go to the ground to search for prey or nesting materials.

may have one to three versions of Part A, two to eight versions of Part B, and six to twelve versions of Part C. Each of these variations is interchangeable, giving the Wood Thrush a wide variety of songs possible by combining the different versions of its three-part song. Some males may sing more than fifty different variations in total, and they usually cycle through many of the different songs during the course of the dawn chorus. Interestingly, male Wood Thrushes removed from the wild at birth are able to sing the A and C portions of the song, but they give only short, slurred versions of the B phase, which indicates that they may learn this part of their song by listening to other Wood Thrushes in the wild.

Ideal habitat for the Wood Thrush includes large blocks (greater than five hundred acres) of relatively unfragmented, mature forest with trees over fifty feet in height, a moderate understory of shrubs and saplings, and a relatively open forest floor with water nearby. Wood Thrushes often feed on the forest floor, where they flip over leaves in search of prey. Common food items include beetles, spiders, caterpillars, and ants, although they occasionally take prey as large as small salamanders. In late summer, the birds also eat a variety of fruit, including spicebush, blueberry, holly, grapes, jack-in-the-pulpit, Virginia creeper, and dogwood.

Although the Wood Thrush will sometimes attempt to nest in smaller, fragmented woodlots, these habitats are often "sinks" where the birds may nest, but they are not typically able to produce as many young as in higher-quality habitats. It is possible that increased nest parasitism from the Brown-headed Cowbird in the fragmented woodlands may explain lower reproductive success. One study published in the *Wilson Bulletin* reported a cowbird parasitism rate for Wood Thrush nests in the Midwest to be 42.1 percent. However, other sources indicate that in some Midwestern forests with high fragmentation, nearly every Wood Thrush nest is parasitized by cowbirds. Despite these impacts, the role of forest fragmentation on the Wood Thrush is more complex. In some cases, Wood Thrush nestlings seem to grow faster when the nest is placed near some type of disturbance (e.g., clear-cutting, power line) within a larger forest block. It is thought the faster growth rate is due to higher food production in these sunny openings than in the surrounding mature forest.

Identification. The Wood Thrush has a body shape similar to the American Robin but is slightly smaller. The back is a *rich reddish brown*, with brighter red hues at the nape. The belly is white with large, *circular dark spots*. Most birds show at least a partial white eye ring. The similar Hermit Thrush has the rich red color only on its tail and the rest of its back and wings are light brown. The Hermit Thrush's spots are also smaller and less numerous than those of the Wood Thrush. The larger Brown Thrasher has a longer tail than the Wood Thrush and streaks instead of spots on the breast.

Vocalizations. The song is a beautiful, flutelike *ee-oo-lay* usually given while perched on a bare branch. The call is a sharp *pit-pit-pit* that can be quite loud and forceful.

Nesting. Nest height varies, but the nest is often placed in a sapling less than ten feet off the ground. Species commonly used for nesting include flowering dogwood, spicebush, and several oak species. The female lays three to four pale greenish-blue eggs. The young fledge within twelve days after hatching and are tended by both parents. Multiple nests per year are usually attempted.

Matt Williams

23 Evening Grosbeak
(*Coccothraustes vespertinus*)

STATUS:
  2014 NABCI Yellow Watch List, 2016 NABCI
  Watch List, 2016 PIF Watch List

ESTIMATED POPULATION TREND:
  −92% during the period 1970–2014

LENGTH: 7"

Evening Grosbeak, January, Minnesota: In shades of charcoal
and gold, the male Evening Grosbeak is a spectacular bird.

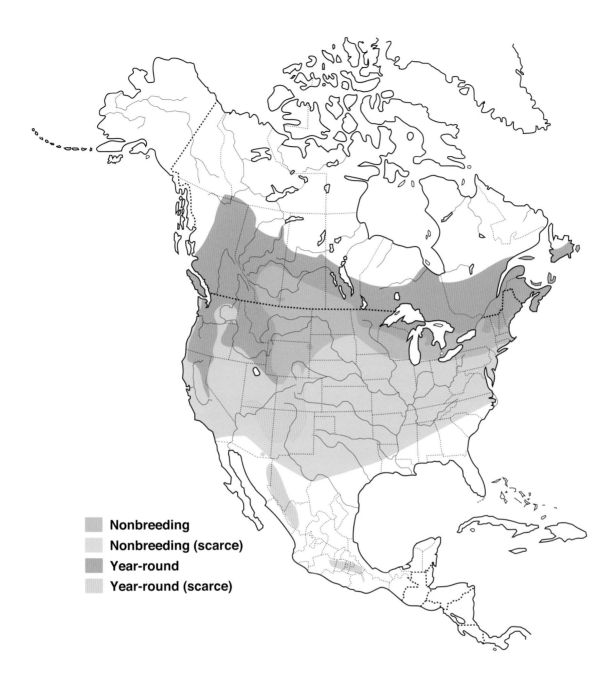

Nonbreeding
Nonbreeding (scarce)
Year-round
Year-round (scarce)

Species Account. Evening Grosbeaks are some of the most beautiful birds in the Midwest. Males have bright lemon-yellow bellies with charcoal heads and black wings with large white wing patches that flash when the birds are in flight. The gold, curved eyebrow stripe is reminiscent of the winged football helmet of the University of Michigan Wolverines. Females are much more muted, with soft grays and yellowish-green tints. Both sexes sport massive beaks that are used for cracking open the maple, ash, box elder, and other seeds that make up a huge portion of the birds' diet.

Evening Grosbeak, January, Minnesota: Female Evening Grosbeaks share the males' enormous bills but are more subtly colored in shades of tan with yellow-green patches on the napes of their necks.

Northern Minnesota, Wisconsin, and Michigan are some of the only places in the United States outside of New England, where these birds are resident east of the Rocky Mountains—although all Midwestern states can have Evening Grosbeak flocks arrive during the winter. In most winters, Evening Grosbeaks stay primarily in the evergreens of the northern latitudes. However, during irruption years, Evening Grosbeaks have migrated to states as far south as Texas, Mississippi, and Alabama in search of food. These irruptions have become smaller and less frequent in recent years as the birds' population has suffered decline. Interestingly, winter flocks in the Northeast tend to have higher percentages of males, whereas flocks farther south tend to have more females. Winter flocks of Evening Grosbeaks may reach numbers as high as several hundred birds, although flocks of ten to forty are more common. Winter flocks are often attracted to roadsides, where they consume road salt used in deicing. In some cases, thousands of Evening Grosbeaks have been killed by vehicles along short stretches of roads where they are feeding on salt.

The Evening Grosbeak historically was very uncommon or absent in the east and was considered a western species until around 1900. The species first reached Rhode Island in the winter of 1910–1911, and it had become a regular winter visitor across much of New England by the 1920s. It is possible that the planting of ornamental trees and the popularity of winter bird feeding helped this species expand its range to the east. The population has always been somewhat cyclical, and overall numbers of the birds may be closely tied to spruce budworm outbreaks—a favorite food source during the breeding season.

According to Breeding Bird Survey data from the U.S. Geological Survey, the Evening Grosbeak has suffered population declines during the past thirty years as high as any other species included in this book—although the birds occur on so few routes that it is hard to draw firm conclusions about population trends. Results from Audubon's Christmas Bird Count (CBC) reflect a similarly steep drop. In 1984, observers in the United States recorded 89,054 Evening Grosbeaks during the CBC. By 2012, only 2,436 birds were reported. Reasons for the decline are unclear, but they may be related to disease outbreaks such as West Nile virus, or changing forest practices that include pesticide use to control spruce budworm outbreaks, among other factors.

Identification. Evening Grosbeaks are large, stocky finches with enormous beaks useful for crushing seeds. Males have *yellow, curved stripes from the beak that trail back over the eyes*, lemon-yellow underparts with charcoal-colored heads, and black wings with large white wing patches that are conspicuous in flight. Females and immature birds are a much softer, muted gray with greenish-yellow neck and flanks and black wings with smaller white patches.

Vocalizations. The Evening Grosbeak is somewhat unusual in that it does not have a song that it uses to advertise for a mate or to defend its territory. The call notes are a shrill, piercing *cleer*. Some of the calls of the Evening Grosbeak can sound similar to the noises of House Sparrows.

Nesting. During courtship the male displays with raised tail and head, as well as lowered, vibrating wings. He will also feed the female and may continue to do so while she is incubating the three to four blue-green eggs speckled with darker colors. The nest, built by the female, is a loose cup generally placed between twenty and sixty feet above the ground. Evening Grosbeaks can produce two broods per year when conditions are good.

Matt Williams

Evening Grosbeak, January, Minnesota: In flight, Evening Grosbeaks reveal large white wing patches near the base of the wing.

24 Pine Siskin
(*Spinus pinus*)

STATUS:
  Common Bird in Steep Decline

ESTIMATED POPULATION TREND:
  −90% during the period 1966–2014

LENGTH: 5"

Pine Siskin, January, Indiana: During invasion years Pine Siskins can be seen in good numbers across the Midwest, sometimes mixing with flocks of American Goldfinches.

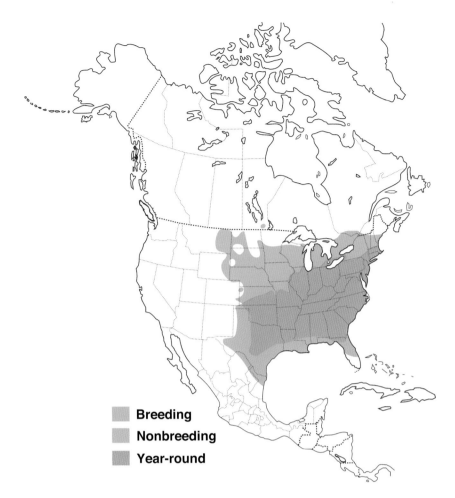

Breeding

Nonbreeding

Year-round

Species Account. Field Sparrows are common breeding birds in Midwest upland grasslands, but populations are dropping rapidly. They breed from central Minnesota, northern Wisconsin, and northern Michigan south throughout the region and farther south to northern Florida and central Texas; they are relatively scarce at the northern limit of their range in the upper Great Lakes states and most common in Missouri, southern Illinois, southern Indiana, and southern Ohio. Nearly half the breeding population is found in the Midwest and upper South, including Kentucky and Tennessee. However, even with this wide distribution they are not familiar birds to many, as they rarely nest in cities or suburbs. Look for this sparrow in old fields with scattered shrub and trees and other habitats with similar structure such as pine plantations, abandoned farms, rights of way with grasslands, and jack pine barrens. They feed on seeds, particularly grass seeds, and insects. Males establish territories in April. The song, which starts as a slow trill, gradually accelerating to a rapid trill, attracts females, who arrive about two weeks after males. By late July to early August most breeding is completed. Birds migrate in late September and October to wintering areas south of the Ohio River in the southeastern United States and northeastern Mexico. Here small flocks of Field Sparrows consume seeds in abandoned agricultural fields and pastures, sometimes in the company of other species of sparrows.

As grasslands are lost to development and agriculture, and by succession to forested habitats, the amount of habitat for Field Sparrows and associated species is shrinking, and thus the marked decline in numbers of Field Sparrows. Protection and continued management of grasslands will be necessary to maintain the current population of Field Sparrows, which was estimated to be about 9 million birds in 2014. Prairie protection and management, programs designed to create Northern Bobwhite and Ring-necked Pheasant habitat, and U.S. Department of Agriculture farm-bill programs that favor conversion of agricultural lands to grasslands all should benefit Field Sparrows.

Identification. Male and female Field Sparrows have similar plumage. The brownish-rufous back is streaked, the cap and crown is rufous, and the undersides are unstreaked and clear gray. No other sparrow with a rusty crown and nape in this region also has a *pink bill and legs*. Also distinctive, but sometimes less conspicuous than the pink bill, is a complete, white eye ring. They are relatively small sparrows and have a proportionately long tail. Juveniles are streaked below. In contrast, Chipping Sparrows have a white eye line bordered by a narrow black eye line; during the breeding season Chipping Sparrows tend to be in areas with short grass and scattered conifers. Swamp Sparrows also are clear gray below and have a rusty cap but also have rusty flanks; Swamp Sparrows, though, are found exclusively in wetlands during the breeding season and not in the upland old fields preferred by Field Sparrows. Both Chipping and Swamp Sparrows lack the white eye ring and pink bill and legs that characterize Field Sparrows.

Vocalizations. The "bouncing ball" song of the Field Sparrow is a series of notes that accelerate as the song progresses. As with other songbirds, the song is learned but few individuals have songs that do not have this characteristic pattern. Field Sparrows have a variety of call notes that take considerable practice to distinguish from call notes of other sparrows.

Nesting. Once paired, females build nests on the ground early in the nesting season, mid-May through early June, but by midsummer most nests are in shrubs. A clutch of four small, speckled eggs is common and two broods of young may be raised during a breeding season. Both parents feed the young with females feeding at higher rates than males. Brown-headed Cowbird parasitism varies considerably in different parts of the Midwest, with rates of parasitism as low as 11 percent in parts of Missouri and Illinois to as high as 80 percent in some areas of Iowa. Field Sparrows are poor hosts for cowbirds, as many abandon their nests once they have been parasitized. Snakes often feed on eggs and nestlings.

Dave Ewert

Field Sparrow, April, Indiana: The Field Sparrow is a bird of brushy overgrown pastures, shrub lands, and fencerows.

27 Grasshopper Sparrow
(*Ammodramus savannarum*)

STATUS:
Common Bird in Steep Decline, State Special Concern (Michigan)

ESTIMATED POPULATION TREND:
−75% during the period 1966–2014

LENGTH: 5"

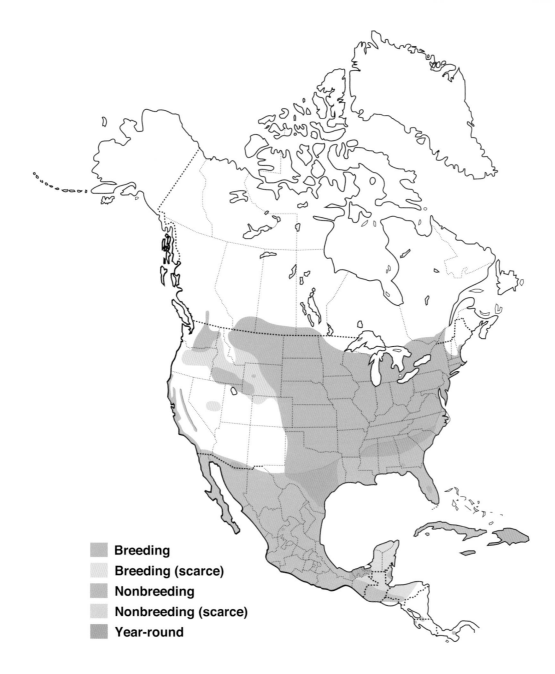

Breeding
Breeding (scarce)
Nonbreeding
Nonbreeding (scarce)
Year-round

Species Account. The Grasshopper Sparrow is a small, relatively nondescript sparrow of open fields and grasslands that appears flat headed and short tailed. The birds generally prefer grasslands with patchy bare areas and few shrubs. Hayfields, prairies, and pasture are favored habitats—especially drier upland sites. Whether the bird was named for its buzzy, insectlike song or for its diet preferences appears to be a matter of debate, but either is appropriate. Like other members of the genus *Ammodramus*, the Grasshopper Sparrow is relatively inconspicuous, spending most of its time on or near the ground and preferring to escape from danger by scurrying through the vegetation rather than flying.

Facing, Grasshopper Sparrow, July, South Dakota: The Grasshopper Sparrow lives in upland grasslands, where it often gives its insectlike song from an exposed perch.

Grasshopper Sparrow, July, South Dakota: Juvenile Grasshopper
Sparrows show a band of fine streaking across the breast.

The range of the Grasshopper Sparrow is surprisingly widespread, and birds are
present in suitable habitat all the way from the East Coast to California. Distribution
of these birds has changed over time in response to land use. There was likely some
range expansion in response to the clearing of eastern forests; however, populations
have overall been strongly trending down in more recent decades, likely due to the
conversion of grasslands for agriculture and development. At present, the bulk of the
population occurs in the remaining grasslands of the Midwest and Great Plains.

In all, there are twelve recognized subspecies—four of which occur in the United
States. The U.S. subspecies include the Eastern Grasshopper Sparrow (*A. savannarum
pratensis*), which occurs as far west as Wisconsin and Oklahoma. The Western Grasshopper Sparrow (*A. savannarum perpallidus*) is present in the northwestern United
States and portions of southern Canada and overlaps with the range of the eastern
subspecies in the Midwest. The Arizona subspecies (*A. savannarum ammolegus*) is
present in Arizona, New Mexico, and portions of Mexico. The Florida subspecies
of Grasshopper Sparrow (*A. savannarum floridanus*) is now only found near Lake
Okeechobee and in central Osceola County, Florida. With a population of fewer than
two hundred birds, this subspecies is one of the rarest birds in the continental United

Endangered and Disappearing Birds of the Midwest

States. Captive breeding efforts are under way in an attempt to prevent extinction. Four other subspecies of Grasshopper Sparrow occur from Mexico south to Ecuador, and an additional four subspecies are present in the Caribbean.

After wintering in the southern tier of states, Grasshopper Sparrows begin to return to the Midwest in late April and early May. May and June are the primary months for nesting and are usually the time of year when Grasshopper Sparrows are most easily located by listening for their song, which is often delivered from a perch on a taller weed stalk or fence post. Most birds migrate south in September and October, but occasionally this sparrow can be found in the Midwest into the month of November.

The diet of the Grasshopper Sparrow is varied, but during the summer months, insects such as grasshoppers, beetles, ants, caterpillars, and centipedes make up the bulk of prey items. In winter, seeds from grasses and weeds become more important food sources. Grasshopper Sparrows forage alone, on the ground where they search for prey from the soil or plant stems.

Identification. The Grasshopper Sparrow is a *small, buffy, flat-headed, short-tailed* sparrow of open grasslands. Adults are clear breasted or at most only faintly streaked below. The crown is dark brown with a pale stripe through the middle. Known to Audubon as the Yellow-winged Bunting, some birds do show yellow at the bend of the closed wing as well as yellow or gold lores. Juvenile birds appear similar to adults but show a band of faint streaks across the breast. Similar species include the LeConte's Sparrow and Henslow's Sparrow; however, both of these species have streaking on the breast or flanks that is absent on adult Grasshopper Sparrows. LeConte's Sparrows are more orange than Grasshopper Sparrows, and Henslow's Sparrows have a patch of greenish olive on their faces that is absent in Grasshopper Sparrows.

Vocalizations. The song of the Grasshopper Sparrow is high and insectlike. The song *kip-kip zeeeee* begins with two to three short notes followed by a long buzz. The pitch is high enough to be almost inaudible for some. Call notes are short, high, burry squeaks.

Nesting. Nests of Grasshopper Sparrows are extremely difficult to locate and are usually situated at the base of a clump of grass. Often they have a dome of overhanging grasses with a side entrance to the nest. The nest is a cup constructed of fine grasses, rootlets, and fur with the lip of the cup at ground level. Four to five eggs are generally laid. Eggs are white with brown or reddish speckles. Incubation is done by the female alone. The female also tends the young, but the male helps respond to predators near the nest. Adult birds prepare grasshoppers by shaking the legs off before feeding to the young.

Matt Williams

Grasshopper Sparrow, July, South Dakota: The Grasshopper Sparrow often shows yellow lores and yellow patches at the bend in the wing.

28 Henslow's Sparrow
(*Ammodramus henslowii*)

STATUS:

> 2014 NABCI Red Watch List, 2016 NABCI Watch List, IUCN Near Threatened, State Special Concern (Ohio), State Threatened (Iowa, Wisconsin), State Endangered (Indiana, Michigan, Minnesota)

ESTIMATED POPULATION TREND:

> Significant declines have occurred, with some authors suggesting drops as high as –7.5% per year from 1966 to 2000. However, these declines may be at least partially offset by the creation of the Conservation Reserve Program, which has increased suitable habitat for this species.

LENGTH: 5"

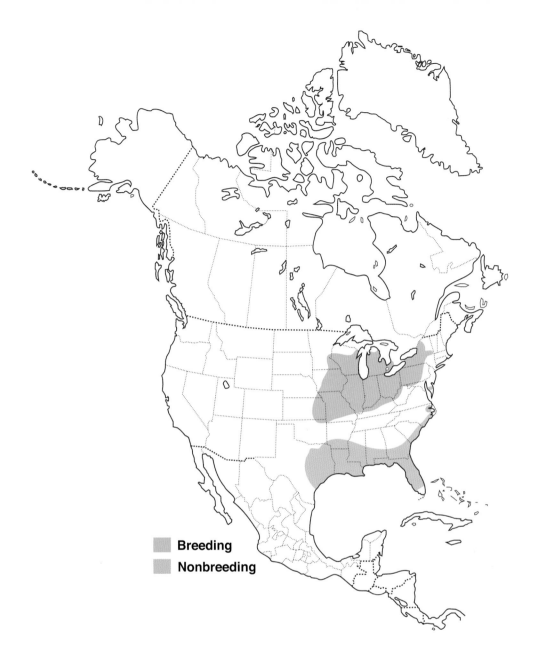

Breeding
Nonbreeding

Species Account. There is no easy way to see Henslow's Sparrows. First of all, the species has declined to the point that it is now largely limited to a relatively few remaining chunks of prairies and wet meadows of sufficient size and quality to support a population. To make finding Henslow's Sparrows even more difficult, the birds are skulkers that prefer to stay close to the ground in thick vegetation. In fact, on the wintering grounds along the Gulf Coast, observers literally spread out in a line and beat the grasses with poles or sticks to catch a fleeting glimpse of a bird in flight and survey the population. Undoubtedly, the best time to see a Henslow's Sparrow is during the breeding season, when the males occasionally fly to the top of a weed stalk to deliver their song, but even then it is not easy to see this bird well. The song itself is a short

Facing, Henslow's Sparrow, April, Indiana: Henslow's Sparrows have a flat-headed appearance and olive coloration on the head, with chestnut and black markings on the back.

Henslow's Sparrow, April, Indiana: The Henslow's Sparrow calls are soft and high pitched, sounding more like an insect than a bird.

and weak *ss-lick* that sounds more like an insect than a bird. The short duration, high pitch, and weakness in volume all combine to make the direction and distance to the singer difficult to judge. However, when a combination of hard work, perseverance, and luck pay off, the reward of seeing this bird is well worth it. The muted shades of olive, buff, and rust of the Henslow's have a subtle beauty when seen in good light that is made all the more special by knowing how few in number the watchers are who get to soak in a satisfying view of a Henslow's Sparrow.

Henslow's once bred across the tallgrass prairies of the Midwest and also in the coastal marshes of the Eastern Seaboard, although today that range is largely limited to a narrow band stretching from eastern Kansas to western New York. The bird was first described to science by John James Audubon from a bird collected in Kentucky in 1820. Audubon named the bird in honor of John Stevens Henslow, a friend and professor of botany at Cambridge University who had helped him to sell subscriptions to his *Birds of North America* during one of Audubon's earlier visits to England.

Endangered and Disappearing Birds of the Midwest

Appropriate management of remaining breeding habitat for the Henslow's Sparrow is a subject of some debate. Prescribed fire as a management tool for the wet grassland habitats the birds prefer is often cast in a negative light because it removes the layer of dead grasses from previous growing seasons. After a fire, Henslow's are often absent for several years before the habitat again becomes sufficiently rank enough for use. However, if fire is completely removed from the system, grasslands quickly become too brushy and are abandoned by the birds. It is likely that in the past when the birds had vast swaths of prairie covering hundreds or even thousands of square miles, a mosaic of microhabitats were available that included different stands of grasses that had burned at different intervals. In that scenario, some suitable habitat was always available that would meet the Henslow's needs. Now, when remaining prairie habitat is largely available only in small, isolated chunks, it is much more difficult to replicate this mosaic today.

Henslow's Sparrows migrate back to their breeding grounds in the Midwest beginning in April. This date is supported by the report of thirty-two dead Henslow's Sparrows found along the shoreline of Lake Michigan following a heavy storm on April 16, 1960. Males are often reported singing on territories by mid-May, and the birds likely leave our area headed south to their wintering grounds by September and October. A handful of birds have been reported on Christmas Bird Counts from the Midwest during December, but it seems very unusual for the birds to linger that late in the year.

Identification. The Henslow's Sparrow appears *large billed and large headed* for its body size. The face has an *olive cast* that extends to the nape of the neck. There is a white eye ring and a brown streak behind the eye. There are fine, dark streaks confined to a band across the breast and extending down the flanks. The back appears scaly because of the white edging on some feathers, and blends rufous, black, and rich tan colorations. Male and female are identical. In our region, the Henslow's Sparrow is most likely to be confused with the Grasshopper Sparrow, which lacks the black streaks on the breast and olive cast to the face.

Vocalizations. The song is a weak, insectlike, two-part *ss-lick* that has been described as a "feeble hiccup." Call notes are a high, sharp *tsik* note.

Nesting. The nest is a deep cup of grasses and leaves sometimes lined with fur that is built within twenty inches of the ground, often at the base of a tuft of grass. The nest is built solely by the female in four to six days. The clutch typically includes three to five glossy white eggs heavily marked with reddish brown. Several pairs may nest in close proximity to each other in a loose colony.

Matt Williams

29 Bobolink
(*Dolichonyx oryzivorus*)

STATUS:
  2014 NABCI Yellow Watch List, 2016 NABCI Watch List,
  2016 PIF Watch List, State Special Concern (Ohio)

ESTIMATED POPULATION TREND:
  –65% during the period 1966–2015

LENGTH: 7"

Bobolink, July, South Dakota: The female Bobolink is much more drab and sparrow-like in coloration than her mate, with his black-and-white "tuxedo" plumage.

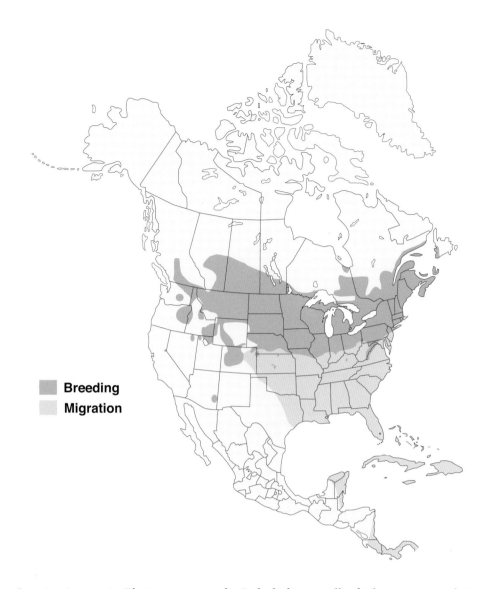

Breeding

Migration

Species Account. Thirty years ago, the Bobolink was still a fairly common sight in the Midwest. In the spring, hayfields and prairie remnants would be alive with the bubbling, gurgling, rollicking song of male Bobolinks flying low over the vegetation with stiff wingbeats, as the birds declared their domain. While many birds have darker coloration on their backs and lighter colors on their bellies, the male Bobolink turns this convention on its head with his jet-black belly that contrasts strikingly with the white on his rump, wings, and back. The lemony-buff nape tops off the ensemble, making the Bobolink one of the more beautiful birds in the blackbird family.

Despite weighing only a couple of ounces, the Bobolink is an accomplished world traveler. Bobolinks breed across the upper Midwest and Great Plains, and their migration takes them across many miles of open ocean as they cross the Gulf of Mexico and the Caribbean and finally reach wintering grounds as far south as Argentina. In all, a Bobolink may travel the equivalent distance of four to five times around the circumference of the earth in their lifetime.

Bobolink, June, Indiana: The male Bobolink is becoming an increasingly rare sight across Midwestern prairies and hayfields. Their bubbling song carries for long distances in the spring and is often given in flight.

While Bobolinks are still common in places like the Great Plains, population numbers overall, especially in the Midwest, have steeply declined in recent decades. According to Breeding Bird Survey data, declines of over 80 percent in Iowa and Ohio and more than 90 percent in Illinois have occurred in the past fifty years. There may be several factors behind the declines. In recent decades, agriculture has undergone intensification. Where there was once a diversity of hayfields, pastures, small grains,

Endangered and Disappearing Birds of the Midwest

orchards, and row crops, today we see a system in place that has converted much of the hay and pasture lands to row crop agriculture consisting primarily of corn and soybean fields. For example, in Illinois, where Bobolink declines are exceptionally steep, corn and soybeans have gone from covering about 35 percent of the landscape in 1950 to covering almost 60 percent today—largely at the expense of pasture and hayfields that may have been habitat for Bobolinks. In addition, the hayfields that remain are being hayed so frequently that few nests or nestlings have a chance to survive before the next cutting.

On the wintering grounds, conditions are apparently not much better. Bobolinks are considered by rice farmers to be a pest in Bolivia and other South American countries, where flocks of 150,000 birds have been recorded. Either intentionally or unintentionally, it appears that Bobolinks are ingesting significant levels of pesticides while on the wintering grounds. One study in Bolivia showed that 40 percent of Bobolinks had some level of pesticides in their blood, and some at lethal levels. In Colombia, Cuba, and Venezuela, Bobolinks are also trapped as a nuisance by rice farmers or to be sold into the pet trade.

Identification. During the breeding season, the male is distinctive with *all-black underparts contrasting sharply with a striking white and black pattern on the back and rump, topped off with a golden nape patch.* During the rest of the year, he takes on the more sparrowlike coloration of the female, who bears chocolate-brown streaking on the flanks, crown, and through the eye, with a buffy unmarked breast. In this plumage, Bobolinks can be confused with Grasshopper Sparrows, which lack the strong stripe through the eye of the Bobolink and are smaller in size.

Vocalizations. Described by various authors as "bubbling" or "tinkling," the male's song is a complex series of electronic-sounding buzzes and chattering. In tone, the song is somewhat similar to that of the Red-winged Blackbird but is more rambling and random. Males and females also give *chunk* or *pink* call notes to communicate year-round.

Nesting. The female builds her nest within one to two days with no help from the male. She builds on the ground, typically at the base of a clump of vegetation. She lays between three and seven white eggs speckled with brown with a darker ring toward one end. Incubation lasts only ten to eleven days, and the young are fed an exclusive diet of high-protein insects.

Matt Williams

30 Eastern Meadowlark
(*Sturnella magna*)

STATUS:
Common Bird in Steep Decline

ESTIMATED POPULATION TREND:
−89% during the period 1966–2015

LENGTH: 9.5"

Eastern Meadowlark, March, Indiana: Eastern Meadowlarks have white malar stripes, whereas Western Meadowlarks show yellow malar stripes. However, the two are so similar that it is best to distinguish them by song if possible.

Breeding
Nonbreeding
Year-round

Species Account. If the Wood Thrush is the master singer amongst all the woodland birds, then perhaps the Eastern Meadowlark should hold that title for the grassland birds. A single male can sing more than one hundred different variations of its song. Meadowlarks have even been known to sing in the winter on warmer days. While many grassland birds make insectlike trills or other rather unimpressive songs, the Eastern Meadowlark sings loud, clear, whistled phrases that carry across the open grasslands that are home to this beautiful bird. While standing upright, the Eastern Meadowlark is beautiful indeed, with a bright lemon-yellow breast and a bold black chevron across its chest. However, when danger approaches, the birds virtually disappear. By simply laying down in the grass to cover their bright colors, the birds' supremely camouflaged black-and-brown dappled backs blend in almost perfectly with their surroundings, making them nearly invisible.

Eastern Meadowlark, April, Texas: The Eastern Meadowlark nests
in grasslands across the eastern half of the country and is distinctive
with its yellow breast and black *V* across the chest.

Eastern Meadowlarks breed in grasslands across the entire United States east of the
Mississippi River and farther west across portions of the Great Plains. A separate race
of Eastern Meadowlark known as Lilian's Meadowlark breeds in desert grasslands of
the Southwest. Some meadowlarks live even further south across portions of Mexico
and into South America. Across much of the Midwest, the range of the Eastern Meadowlark overlaps that of the Western Meadowlark. The two are very similar in appearance, and the best way to separate them is by song. The songs are different enough that
even where the ranges overlap, the two species rarely interbreed. In winter, Eastern
Meadowlarks depart from a good portion of the Midwest, although some remain in
southern Illinois, Indiana, and Ohio throughout the year. Across Michigan, Wisconsin,
Iowa, and Minnesota, they are one of the earliest migrants in the spring, with some
returning as early as February.

Endangered and Disappearing Birds of the Midwest

Eastern Meadowlarks' primary prey items include crickets, grasshoppers, and caterpillars. Meadowlarks sometimes stick their closed beak into the ground and then open the beak to disturb the soil in an effort to seek out grubs and earthworms. Meadowlarks nest in prairies, hayfields, pastures, grasslands, and even at airports. They appear to be more tolerant of habitat fragmentation than some other grassland birds, in that they will sometimes nest in chunks of habitat as small as six acres in size. The female alone builds the nest over a four- to eight-day period. Some nests have roofs and entrance tunnels made of finely woven grasses.

Although there are an estimated 30 million Eastern Meadowlarks that remain today, that number reflects a nearly 90 percent drop in the overall population since 1966. It is possible that the decline can be attributed to hayfields and pastures being converted to more intensive row-crop agriculture. Practices like early haying and mowing destroys nests and nestlings, and also takes a toll on the population.

Identification. The Eastern Meadowlark is a *chunky, stout-looking bird*. In flight, the wingbeats are stiff and shallow, and the birds also glide often during flight. Meadowlarks are *bright yellow on the breast with a black* V *across the chest*. The back is mottled black and brown. The bill is rather long, and in flight they show bright white on the outer parts of the tail. Western Meadowlarks are very similar and are difficult to tell apart in the field unless they sing. Eastern Meadowlarks generally show white malar stripes on the side of the throat, whereas Western Meadowlarks show yellow.

Vocalizations. Eastern Meadowlarks sing with clear, loud whistles that some have described as flutelike. The song is usually in two phrases. They also give a harsh rattling call.

Nesting. Nesting takes place in prairies, old fields, hayfields, and agricultural fields. Nests are built on the ground and are rather elaborate structures with roofs and entrance tunnels. Males are polygamous and may have two or three females that nest on their territory. The female lays three to five smooth, glossy-white eggs speckled with shades of chestnut or purple brown. Eastern Meadowlarks tend to be double brooded and may replace lost clutches.

Matt Williams

31 Golden-winged Warbler
(*Vermivora chrysoptera*)

STATUS:

2014 NABCI Yellow Watch List, 2016 NABCI Watch List, 2016 PIF Watch List, IUCN Near Threatened, State Endangered (Indiana)

CONTINENTAL POPULATION TREND SINCE 1966:

−68% during the period 1966–2014

LENGTH: 4.5"

Golden-winged Warbler, June, Michigan: The Golden-winged Warbler has wing bars that are a brilliant gold—unlike any other warbler.

Breeding
Migration
Winter

Species Account. The Golden-winged Warbler is a much sought-after species, with throngs of anxious binocular-toting birders jamming the boardwalks and paths at the popular migrant traps whenever one is seen in the Midwest during spring migration. In addition to their rarity, their beautiful, subtle, charcoal-gray plumage highlighted with brilliant golden yellow on the crown and wing always attracts a crowd of enthusiastic observers. The black face and throat patch, along with their habit of hanging upside down and probing rolled leaves in search of insects can bring to mind a chickadee, but that thought quickly vanishes when one catches a flash of gold from the crown or wing. Yet despite their popularity, Golden-winged Warblers have been in steep decline for decades, and they are now likely one of the birds with the smallest population size that has not yet been federally listed.

Blue-winged Warbler (for comparison): Hybrids of the Blue-winged and Golden-winged Warbler are separated into two major types: Brewster's Warblers have the facial pattern of the Blue-winged Warbler and the overall coloration of a Golden-winged Warbler, while Lawrence's Warblers have the facial pattern of a Golden-winged Warbler but the golden body coloration of the Blue-winged Warbler.

Among the reasons for the decline of the Golden-winged Warbler are several themes common to many species in this book. Loss of habitat, as is so often the case, is surely among the most important. Like many birds with rapidly declining populations, Golden-winged Warblers need early successional habitat. This patchy, shrubby habitat intermixed with more mature deciduous woodlands was associated in the past with recent wildfires, areas flooded by beavers, and abandoned farmlands, along with shrubby wetlands like bogs and fens. As these habitats have grown up to mature forests, or have been drained in the case of wetlands, less and less appropriate habitat has remained to support Golden-winged Warblers. In some cases, the wetlands that do remain have been taken over by phragmites and other nonnative invasive species that have altered the habitat and made it unsuitable for nesting. Brown-headed Cowbirds also have played a role in reducing the Golden-winged Warbler populations, with one study finding a 17 percent reduction in productivity for Golden-winged Warblers because of nest parasitism.

However, there is another reason behind the decline of the Golden-winged Warbler that is not as common or as obvious. Golden-winged Warblers apparently are being outcompeted and absorbed by a growing population of the closely related Blue-winged Warbler. As the Blue-winged Warblers have expanded their range northward, Golden-winged Warblers appear to be losing ground and are themselves being pushed out of more southerly habitats, leaving their last strongholds in more northern locations. Studies have shown that once Blue-winged Warblers invade an area, the Golden-winged Warblers disappear from the area in as few as fifty years. This may be in part because the two species compete for similar resources. However, the two species do breed together and produce viable, hybrid offspring known as Brewster's Warbler or Lawrence's Warbler depending on their physical characteristics. As the hybrid offspring breed with a pure parent species, the genes distinguishing the two species become increasingly blurred. Overall, though, more of the Blue-winged Warbler genes are ending up in the Golden-winged Warbler population. Today, only a small portion of the Golden-winged Warbler population is genetically pure, primarily in Manitoba, Canada. Even birds that appear to be pure Golden-winged Warblers on the basis of their physical appearance often have traces of Blue-winged Warbler genes. Although the reasons for the domination of Blue-winged Warbler genes are not clear, some studies have shown that Golden-winged Warblers are much more likely to breed with hybrid offspring than are Blue-winged Warblers, which could be playing a role in the overall gene flow between the species.

Recent surveys have shown a 98 percent decline in the Golden-winged Warbler populations in the Adirondack Mountains. In other areas, the Golden-winged Warbler has been completely lost as a breeding bird. Today, the states of Michigan, Wisconsin, and Minnesota are the last stronghold for this species, with as much as 95 percent of the global breeding population in this part of the Midwest (including the birds that breed in a small corner of neighboring Manitoba). Approximately 50 percent of the remaining population breeds in Minnesota alone.

Fortunately, a number of institutions and conservation organizations have come together to create the Golden-winged Warbler Working Group. This group has written a conservation plan that details actions that need to be taken to increase the Golden-winged Warbler's chances for survival. The Midwest certainly has a critical role to play in the future of this beautiful songbird.

Identification. The male Golden-winged Warbler has a *jet-black cheek patch and bib* with contrasting white surrounding the black cheek. The breast and underparts are whitish gray, and the back is a steel-gray color with a *gold patch on the wing and on the crown*. The female has similar coloring, but with dark charcoal patches on the throat and cheek instead of black, and less intense gold on the crown. The Chestnut-sided Warbler breeds in similar habitat and also has a golden crown, but it lacks the bold black bib and golden wing patch of the Golden-winged Warbler. The hybrid Brewster's Warbler has the overall coloration of the Golden-winged Warbler with the facial pattern of the Blue-winged Warbler, whereas the Lawrence's Warbler has the overall coloration of the Blue-winged Warbler with the facial pattern of the Golden-winged Warbler. Some variation in these hybrids is possible.

Vocalizations. The male gives a slow, buzzy *bee bzzzz bzzzz*. The first note is higher than the subsequent notes.

Nesting. Golden-winged Warblers nest on the ground, laying three to six pale eggs lightly marked with fine splotches or streaks toward the larger end. The nest is often at the base of a plant stem. Both parents feed the young at the nest until fledging occurs at approximately ten days of age.

Matt Williams

Facing, Golden-winged Warbler, June, Michigan: The male Golden-winged Warbler (pictured) has a jet-black face and throat patch, whereas the female has a similar pattern that is more charcoal gray than black.

Endangered and Disappearing Birds of the Midwest

155

32 Prothonotary Warbler (*Protonotaria citrea*)

STATUS:

2014 NABCI Yellow Watch List, 2016 NABCI Watch List, 2016 PIF Watch List, State Special Concern (Michigan and Ohio)

ESTIMATED POPULATION TREND:

−42% during the period 1966–2015

LENGTH: 5.5"

Prothonotary Warbler, May, Indiana:
When spread, the tail shows large white patches.

Breeding
Breeding (scarce)
Migration
Nonbreeding

Species Account. Prothonotary Warblers are birds of swampy forests and riparian woodlands. Seeing a brilliant-yellow male Prothonotary Warbler suddenly illuminated by a shaft of sunlight in its dark, shaded habitats is a memorable sight. The word *prothonotary* refers to scribes of the Roman Catholic Church who wore yellow hoods reminiscent of the birds' bright plumage. "Golden swamp warbler" has also been suggested as a name and fits the bird equally well. The Prothonotary Warbler is a bird of the swamps of the southeastern United States, but they do nest as far north as the Midwest and southern Ontario. In the Midwest, the largest numbers of these birds are found in Illinois, Indiana, and Ohio.

Males are the first to return from their wintering grounds in the lowland forest and mangroves along the coasts of Mexico and Central America, arriving in our region in April and early May. Upon arrival, the males quickly begin searching for a suitable nesting cavity—the Prothonotary Warbler is the only cavity-nesting warbler species east of the Mississippi. The birds primarily use old nest sites of other species, especially the Downy Woodpecker. However, they have been reported to occasionally excavate their own nest site with their relatively hefty beak, which is unlike that of other warblers. Still, this is possible only if they can find a suitable location in especially soft and decayed wood. The male will start to carry in nesting material in at least one suitable cavity, which he will show off to prospective females. Once a mate is found, the female will finish constructing the nest.

Nesting cavities are typically over water and five to ten feet up in a dead tree or dead branch. However, nests can be as low as two to three feet above the waterline, which

Prothonotary Warbler, May, Indiana: The female Prothonotary Warbler can be distinguished by a slightly less brilliant gold coloration overall and more olive tones on the head and nape.

makes them susceptible to nest failure from flooding. Parasitism by Brown-headed Cowbirds has also been reported, and some studies have indicated a surprising number of Prothonotary Warbler eggs destroyed by House Wrens, which may compete for similar nest sites. However, the largest cause of population decline for the Prothonotary Warbler is likely loss of habitat due to the draining, filling, and clearing of wooded wetlands.

Prothonotary Warblers are most often encountered by canoers and kayakers or seen along boardwalks traversing flooded forest. They are quite often first located by their ringing *sweet sweet sweet sweet sweet* song, or their metallic-sounding alarm call notes. The birds are active foragers and can be seen landing on half-submerged mossy logs, peeking into crevices, and perching on the side of tree trunks. They often seem rather confiding and tame and sometimes land quite near to those who sit still and wait quietly.

Prothonotary Warbler, May, Indiana: The male Prothonotary Warbler has a golden head, greenish back, and steel-blue wings with a black bill that is heavier than that of most other warbler species.

Identification. Prothonotary Warblers are *brilliant golden yellow* on the heads and chest, with unmarked *bluish-gray wings, a greenish back, and white underparts*. They have a relatively heavy black beak and black feet. Females are similar but less brilliantly marked. Prothonotary Warblers also have white spots on the tail that are visible when the tail is spread during flight. The Blue-winged Warbler is similar but has a small black mask between the beak and eyes, and two white wing bars.

Vocalizations. The song is a ringing, metallic *sweet* note repeated seven to ten times in quick succession. The call note is a metallic-sounding chip.

Nesting. Prothonotary Warblers often nest in snags or dead limbs in trees along rivers, lakes, sloughs, or other bodies of water. Some birds have been reported to use nest boxes and other man-made structures for nesting, including posts, buildings, empty tin cans, mailboxes, and even an old pail on the porch of a cabin by a stream. The nest cup is about two inches wide and is made of roots, bark, moss, lichen, and other plant material. Clutch size is three to seven white eggs with brownish spots, but productivity is thought to be low. A Michigan study showed that only 28 percent of 178 nests studied had at least one chick survive to fledging.

Matt Williams

Prothonotary Warbler, June, Indiana: The song of the male Prothonotary
Warbler is a ringing *sweet sweet sweet sweet sweet sweet sweet*, that is often heard by
kayakers and canoers on streams that have wooded, swampy floodplains.

33 | Kentucky Warbler
(*Geothlypis formosa*)

STATUS:
   2014 NABCI Yellow Watch List, 2016 NABCI Watch List,
   2016 PIF Watch List, State Threatened (Wisconsin)

ESTIMATED POPULATION TREND:
   –36% during the period 1966–2014

LENGTH: 5.25"

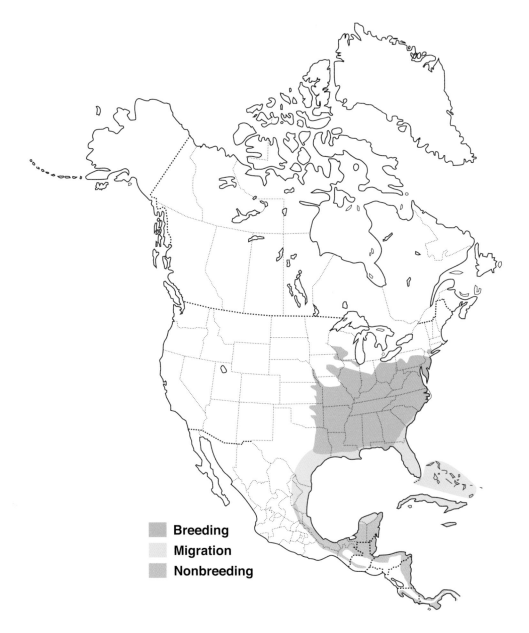

Breeding
Migration
Nonbreeding

Species Account. Like the Mourning Warbler and Connecticut Warbler—two other species that until recently were in the same genus, the Kentucky Warbler is a bird at home on or near the ground. Kentucky Warblers hop on the ground and turn over leaf litter or glean from overhanging leaves to find their prey, which includes spiders, caterpillars, beetles, and ants. During the breeding season, Kentucky Warblers seek out deep woods with a shaded, well-developed, brushy understory. They seem to prefer thickly vegetated ravines and well-shaded slopes. In winter, the birds can be found in humid, forested, lowlands from Mexico, Central America, and the Caribbean, south to Columbia and Venezuela in northern South America. Even in winter, a dense shrub layer in shaded forest habitat appears to be key, and this species seems to be sensitive to forest fragmentation.

Facing, Kentucky Warbler, April, Indiana: The rolling *turdle turdle turdle* song of the Kentucky Warbler can be easily mistaken for that of the Carolina Wren but is a bit mellower in tone.

Kentucky Warbler, April, Indiana: The male Kentucky Warbler has a black crown and face patch, with a yellow line that extends back from the bill and wraps around behind the eye.

In the Midwest, only small numbers of Kentucky Warblers can be found in southern Michigan, Wisconsin, and southeastern Iowa, with no birds regularly found as far north as Minnesota. However, in appropriate habitat across southern Ohio, Indiana, and Illinois, the Kentucky Warbler is still a relatively common nesting bird. Even when the birds are present, though, they are easier to hear than to see because of their preference for rugged terrain and thick understory. Even a singing male can be difficult to locate, as they will sometimes sit very still for minutes at a time when vocalizing, and it can be difficult to judge distance and direction when trying to locate the bird. Many Kentucky Warblers are also missed because their loud, rolling *tur-dle, tur-dle* song is mistaken for that of a Carolina Wren, which sounds quite similar.

Among warblers, the Kentucky Warbler is a relatively early spring migrant. The first birds cross the Gulf of Mexico and can arrive along the U.S. Gulf Coast as early as mid- to late March. In the Midwest, the first spring arrivals are usually found in mid- to late April, with some birds not arriving at the northern edges of their range until early May. Occasionally, birds "overshoot" their normal breeding range and are recorded in

Endangered and Disappearing Birds of the Midwest

Kentucky Warbler, July, Indiana: In late summer, first-year males can be difficult to distinguish from adult female birds. This bird is likely a young male because of the amount of gray in the crown, where an adult female would have more olive tones rather than gray.

the spring farther north. Singing males may be present at these northern locations for a short time, although it is doubtful that breeding occurs in these cases. Fall migration can begin as early as late July, with most birds having left the area by September.

The Kentucky Warbler appears to be a fairly frequent host to nest parasitism by the Brown-headed Cowbird, and lawns and other open space that fragments forest may provide opportunities for the Brown-headed Cowbirds to locate and lay eggs in the nests of Kentucky Warblers. A study of 250 Kentucky Warbler nests in southern Illinois found that the rate of nest parasitism for Kentucky Warbler nests varied from 60 percent of nests near a cowbird feeding area to only 3 percent of Kentucky nests that were about a mile or more away from the cowbird feeding site. The study also showed that older forest stands resulted in lower parasitism rates than in younger forests. In addition to parasitism, deforestation on the wintering grounds and excessive browse due to deer overpopulation resulting in thinner forest understories have been suggested as possible reasons for the birds' decline in recent decades.

Breeding
Migration
Nonbreeding

Species Account. Cape May Warblers are primarily seen during migration by those in the Midwest except those living in the northernmost parts of Minnesota, Wisconsin, and Michigan, where the birds can be found breeding locally in mature spruce-fir forests, especially in extensive bogs and along riparian corridors. Canada is the major breeding area for this boreal species. During the breeding season, Cape May Warblers may be found near the tops of spruces and firs, particularly where there are outbreaks of spruce budworms. In years with many spruce budworms Cape May Warblers can be common, only to disappear or become far less common when the budworm outbreak ceases. During spring migration Cape May Warblers tend to forage in tall trees, including ornamental spruces, but also deciduous trees, especially those in flower, where they may find insects or even nectar, which they extract with their semitubular tongue. Under extremely cold and windy conditions in spring migration, Cape May

Facing, Cape May Warbler, May, Ohio: Female Cape May Warblers are duller than the males and lack the rusty cheek patches. They are much easier to confuse with other warbler species.

Cape May Warbler, September, Indiana: Basic plumage Cape May Warblers in the fall are less colorful but still retain the streaked breast and yellow rump patch that helps with identification.

Warblers are even found hopping on the ground at the edge of pools of water, feeding on emerging midges. Up to fifty individuals may be found in one flock, though such a high number is rare.

During fall migration, Cape May Warblers occupy a wide range of habitats, from shrubby areas to forests, as they seek insects, nectar, and juices from fruits such as grapes. A few Cape May Warblers may remain in the upper Midwest as late as December. Cape May Warblers have an elliptical migration pattern; fall migration is farther east than spring migration, when they primarily migrate west of the Appalachians and east of the Mississippi River. On their Bahamas and West Indian wintering grounds, Cape May Warblers are widely scattered in second-growth or in gardens, especially in areas with many flowers, where they supplement their diet of arthropods with nectar and fruit. Threats to Cape May Warbler populations are poorly known but may include loss of spruce budworm populations to pesticide spraying and loss of mature spruce-fir forests to logging in the breeding grounds.

Endangered and Disappearing Birds of the Midwest

Cape May Warbler, May, Ohio: Male Cape May Warblers in alternate plumage have yellow bellies, rusty cheek patches, and large white wing patches.

Identification. The spring-plumage males are distinctive with their *bright-yellow underparts with bold black streaks*, yellow rump, *rufous cheek patches* and black crown and forehead; females are similarly patterned but less brightly colored and lack rufous cheek patches. Cape May Warblers are more difficult to identify during the fall and winter, as their plumage is much duller and variable. Look for a combination of the following traits: grayish to yellowish below with black streaks, greenish-yellow rump (less conspicuous and discrete than a Yellow-rumped Warbler), a conspicuous to faint yellowish crescent behind the cheek, and a comparatively short tail.

Vocalizations. Cape May Warblers sing high from trees. The song is composed of a series of high, thin, repeated notes and does not carry far. There is individual variation in song that is best appreciated when several males are singing close together. Cape May Warblers also have short, thin call notes.

Nesting. Nests, built of grasses, mosses and small twigs, are placed high in spruces and firs. A typical clutch is six eggs, but up to nine eggs may be laid during spruce budworm years when food is abundant. Females build nests and incubate the eggs but little is known about incubation patterns, nestling periods or fledging.

Dave Ewert

Cape May Warbler, Ohio, May: Cape May Warblers are often attracted to flowering trees, from which they drink nectar to supplement their diet.

36 Cerulean Warbler
(*Setophaga cerulea*)

STATUS:

    2014 NABCI Yellow Watch List, 2016 NABCI Watch List, 2016 PIF Watch List, IUCN Vulnerable, State Special Concern (Minnesota, Ohio), State Threatened (Michigan, Wisconsin, Illinois), State Endangered (Indiana)

ESTIMATED POPULATION TREND:

    −74% during the period 1966–2015

LENGTH: 4.3"

Cerulean Warbler, May, Indiana: Male Cerulean Warblers are easily distinguished by their sky-blue coloration, large white wing bars, and dark necklace across the chest.

Breeding

Migration

Species Account. Unlike so many of the warbler species of the eastern United States, the male Cerulean Warbler has no yellow markings to adorn its plumage. Instead, it lives up to its name and bears a brilliant shade of cerulean blue on its head and back. This sky-blue coloration seems appropriate for a bird that spends so much of its time in the very tops of large, mature trees, forcing observers to stare up into the canopy above to try to catch a glimpse of this tiny warbler. Although missing the brilliant-blue coloration of the male, females also have uniquely beautiful plumage, sporting aqua or sea-green heads and upper backs.

Cerulean Warbler, May, Indiana: The female Cerulean Warbler is also beautiful in shades of aqua instead of the brilliant sky blue of the male. In a way, seeing a female is even more of a treat than the males, who are often easier to find because of their singing.

Although this species has been relatively heavily studied, the exact habitat requirements of the birds remain somewhat debatable. It is generally agreed that Cerulean Warblers require large, intact blocks of mature deciduous forest. Many sources state a minimum size of at least fifty to seventy-five acres of mature forest, with blocks of at least six hundred contiguous acres being preferred. Often, prime habitat for these birds includes steep topography, and sites with streams also seem to be favored. However, there is some evidence that relatively small breaks in the forest canopy may also be important. These openings can be created through storms or the existence of shrubby wetlands within the forest matrix, or they can be deliberately created through different types of timber harvest. Whatever the source, it seems that this structure (small pockets of younger forest within a large matrix of mature deciduous forest with relatively open understory) may be even more critical than other factors such as tree species or soil types. In fact, oak-hickory forests and maple-dominated forests have both been reported to be used for nesting, as have wet, riparian forests and drier, upland sites.

The Cerulean Warbler is one of the most imperiled migrant songbirds in the country and has undergone steep population declines over the past fifty years. Partners in Flight estimates that the population has dropped by more than 70 percent since 1970 and predicts that the remaining population may drop by an additional 50 percent over the next few decades. Habitat loss is likely the biggest cause, with fewer large forest blocks available for nesting in the United States. However, it is the birds' loss of forest habitat in the Andes Mountains of northern South America that may be the biggest driver of population decline, as so much of their wintering habitat has been converted

Cerulean Warbler, May, Indiana: Once one of the most abundant warblers in the Ohio and Mississippi River valleys, Cerulean Warbler numbers have plummeted and will likely drop by another 50 percent over the coming twenty-six years according to Partners in Flight.

to pasture for livestock and for the planting of crops such as rice, cocoa, and coffee. To date, more than 60 percent of the Cerulean Warbler's wintering habitat may have been destroyed. However, recent efforts by the American Bird Conservancy and other groups have helped fund the establishment of forest reserves in that area, as well as the creation of conservation easements to protect remaining forested lands. Reforestation projects have also helped create corridors of habitat between these reserves. More than two hundred private landowners participated in a recent effort to plant shade trees on more than three thousand acres of coffee and cocoa farms in order to provide better habitat corridors between reserves in Colombia.

Identification. The male Cerulean Warbler is nearly unmistakable with a *sky-blue head and back*, and a white belly. There is a *blackish necklace across the chest*, with some dark streaking down the flanks and on the back. The female is *aqua green on the crown and upper back*, with whitish or yellowish underparts and some faint, dark streaking along the sides of the breast and flanks and a white supercilium streak. Both sexes have two strong, white wing bars.

Vocalizations. The song is a rapid series of short buzzy notes followed by a longer, higher-pitched trill.

Nesting. The nest is constructed in the middle to upper canopy of a deciduous tree. Oak, maple, basswood, elm, hickory, sycamore, beech, and tulip trees have all reportedly been used for nesting. Nests can be as low as fifteen feet or as high as ninety feet or more. Nests are constructed of bark, fur, and spider webs among other materials. If a nest fails, the spider webs used in the old nest are often reused in building the new nest. The typical clutch consists of three to five creamy white eggs with brown speckling. When leaving the nest, the female "bungee jumps" by dropping from the nest with closed wings toward the forest floor before finally spreading her wings to fly to her destination. This may be a tactic to avoid detection of the nest location by predators.

Matt Williams

Cerulean Warbler, May, Indiana: The declining population size spurred the creation of the Cerulean Warbler Technical Group in 2001 in an effort to better understand the habitat needs of this species.

37 | Blackpoll Warbler
(*Setophaga striata*)

STATUS:
Common Bird in Steep Decline

ESTIMATED POPULATION TREND:
−92% during the period 1966–2015

LENGTH: 5.25″

Blackpoll Warbler, September, Indiana: In the fall, Blackpoll Warblers can be difficult to tell from Bay-breasted Warblers. Blackpoll Warblers typically have some light coloration on the legs or feet that helps to distinguish them from Bay-breasted Warblers, which usually have dark legs and feet.

Breeding
Migration

Species Account. For humans, running a marathon is an incredible feat that takes physical and mental stamina, determination, and usually months of training. A marathon covers about twenty-six miles and can be run in a time of six hours or less. Now consider the fall migration of the Blackpoll Warbler. The birds nest in boreal forest across much of Canada and as far west as Alaska. They depart their nesting grounds and head east-southeast toward the New England coastline. Upon reaching the Atlantic Coast in New England or in the Maritime Provinces of Canada, they depart on a marathon of their own. These small birds head out over open ocean on a southeasterly course. It is possible that many times their departure coincides with the passage of a cold front, which provides a strong northwesterly tail wind for the journey. Flying southeast, the birds wing their way nonstop to the Caribbean, where they may benefit from trade winds that push them in a southwesterly direction toward the coast of South

Blackpoll Warbler,
May, Ohio: The male
Blackpoll in alternate
plumage has a black
cap, white cheek
patch, and black
streaks on the flanks.

Blackpoll Warbler, May, Ohio: Blackpoll Warbler's straw-colored legs and feet help to distinguish these birds from similar species.

America. The birds that survive this journey will have traveled for eighty to eighty-eight hours straight, and will have covered more than two thousand miles since they began their journey—the longest nonstop open-ocean flight of any songbird in North America. In total, the birds that nest in Alaska will travel as many as five thousand miles before reaching their wintering grounds in the Amazon Basin in Brazil.

To achieve this spectacular migration, Blackpoll Warblers have to consume vast quantities of insects before departing their breeding grounds. Some scientists have described Blackpoll Warblers departing for their fall migration as "meatballs with wings" because of the vast fat reserves the birds pack on. In some cases, Blackpoll Warblers double their body weight before attempting the trip. In addition, the birds absorb nonessential organs in order to maximize the range they are capable of flying.

Blackpoll Warblers are somewhat unusual in that they take different routes during their spring and fall migration. As "elliptical" migrants, Blackpoll Warblers travel farther west on their return trip to their breeding grounds. They cross the western Caribbean, and then travel north through the eastern United States, returning to their boreal-forest breeding grounds in May. This elliptical route means that Blackpoll Warblers are rarely seen in the Midwest in the fall south of the Great Lakes, but they are fairly common across our region during spring migration.

Partners in Flight estimates that there are still tens of millions of Blackpoll Warblers. However, they also estimate that since 1970, we have lost a staggering number—more than 700 million. If you laid the Blackpoll Warblers we have lost end to end you could completely circle the globe—twice. Within the next sixteen years it is predicted that we will lose another 50 percent of the Blackpoll Warblers that are left today.

Identification. In spring, both males and females have grayish backs and flanks with black streaks, white wing bars and bellies, and *yellowish legs and feet.* The female has streaks on the crown and on the side of the throat, whereas the male has a *bold black cap, black stripe at the side of the throat, and a bright-white cheek patch.* In fall, the birds resemble the spring female but have more of a yellowish-olive wash. Fall birds may also have darker legs, but they *typically retain the yellowish color at least on the underside of the feet.* Similar species include the Black-and-white Warbler, but males of that species have black cheek patches rather than the white cheek patch of the Blackpoll. In fall, Blackpolls are difficult to distinguish from the very similar-looking Bay-breasted Warbler. Bay-breasted Warblers tend to have at least some buffy or rusty coloration on the flanks, whereas Blackpoll Warblers are more washed with yellow olive in this area. The color of the feet and legs can be helpful if visible, as Bay-breasted Warblers will always be dark gray or black here.

Vocalizations. The song of the Blackpoll Warbler is as high pitched as that of any warbler—too high to hear for some people. The song is a rapid series of short notes all on one pitch. The volume of the song increases and then later decreases.

Nesting. Blackpoll Warblers breed in boreal forest. Both sexes often return to the same territory, but some males mate with more than one female. The nest is usually next to the trunk of the tree and one to ten feet above the ground. It is made up of twigs, grasses, moss, and lichen. Typical clutch size is four to five cream-colored eggs that are speckled with brown concentrated toward the larger end. The young fledge within twelve days of hatching and are fed by both parents. Blackpoll Warblers occasionally attempt a second brood.

Matt Williams

Bay-breasted Warbler (for comparison), September, Indiana: This bird can be distinguished as a Bay-breasted Warbler because it has some warmer buff hues in the crown and flanks, and because the legs and feet are uniformly dark. When seen from below, the undertail coverts are also buffy, whereas the undertail coverts on Blackpoll Warblers are a clean white.

38 Prairie Warbler
(*Setophaga discolor*)

STATUS:
> 2014 NABCI Yellow Watch List, 2016 NABCI Watch List,
> 2016 PIF Watch List, State Endangered (Michigan)

ESTIMATED POPULATION TREND:
> −66% during the period 1966–2014

LENGTH: 4.3"

Prairie Warbler, September, Indiana: Even during fall migration, the Prairie Warbler is distinctive and fairly easily recognizable.

Breeding
Migration
Nonbreeding
Year-round

Species Account. The Prairie Warbler has a truly misleading name, as it is a bird of shrub lands, brush, and old field habitat. Admittedly, though, "scrub warbler" or "clear-cut warbler" doesn't have quite the same ring as Prairie Warbler. You would be hard pressed to find this bird in true open prairie habitats; rather, it prefers early successional wooded habitats that are often associated with poor soils. The constantly shifting sand dunes around the Great Lakes, overgrown orchards and Christmas-tree farms, shrubby clear-cuts, areas recovering after fires, and old farm fields with patches of shrubs and young trees are all places to look for this species in our region. Disturbed areas such as clear-cuts, burned areas, or abandoned fields are suitable for Prairie Warblers beginning about five years after a disturbance, and they remain in use for roughly ten to twenty years. The birds seem to key in on areas with the right mix of open spaces, dense shrubs, and small trees, along with the absence of a closed canopy of mature trees.

Prairie Warbler, May, Indiana: Female Prairie Warblers have slightly more subdued coloration than the males, with less black in the face.

Facing, Prairie Warbler, June, Indiana: Male Prairie Warblers in alternate plumage have chestnut streaking on their backs and bold black-and-yellow facial patterns.

With the logging of much of the eastern forests, Prairie Warblers enjoyed a range expansion and likely reached peak population numbers in the Midwest sometime in the 1940s and 1950s, during which time they were even recorded nesting as far north as Marquette, Alger, and Schoolcraft Counties in the Upper Peninsula of Michigan. According to Breeding Bird Survey data, however, the Prairie Warbler has suffered significant declines across its range since the 1960s. This decline is likely due to changing forestry practices and fire suppression, which have resulted in a shift toward older forests. Habitat has also been lost in the Caribbean within the wintering range of this species due to development and agriculture, and this may be contributing to the overall declines.

In addition to loss of habitat, there are other factors negatively affecting population numbers. Brown-headed Cowbirds are known to parasitize the nests of Prairie Warblers, forcing Prairie Warbler parents to raise cowbirds instead of their own chicks. In some cases, nest parasitism by Brown-headed Cowbirds will force Prairie Warblers to abandon a nest altogether. In the northern parts of their breeding range, it may not be possible to attempt a second nesting if the first nest fails. Prairie Warblers also

Endangered and Disappearing Birds of the Midwest

seem to suffer unusually high mortality rates, especially as fledglings. Only about 20 percent of Prairie Warbler eggs hatch and result in chicks that survive to leave the nest as fledglings. Of these successful fledglings, 79 percent will perish within their first year of life before returning to the breeding grounds as adults. Natural predators include chipmunks, snakes, and other birds. Despite all these factors, Prairie Warblers are still fairly common birds in the southern portions of our region, with good numbers in southern Indiana, and Ohio, some populations in southern Illinois, and a few scattered breeding areas in the dunes around the Great Lakes and elsewhere.

Facing, Prairie Warbler, April, Indiana: Prairie Warblers are fairly early migrants in spring, returning to their breeding grounds in the Midwest as early as mid-April.

Identification. Males are *bright lemon yellow on the face, throat, breast and underparts.* They have bold, black markings on the flanks. A black line runs through the eye, and *a black malar stripe extends from the corner of the beak down the side of the throat.* The back is an olive green with chestnut streaks on the upper back. The female is similar looking but with muted colors. There are two very faint wing bars. Prairie Warblers are "tail-wagging" warblers, meaning that they habitually pump their tails up and down while they are perched. Similar species include the Magnolia Warbler (with a darker back and much more white on the wing) and Kirtland's Warbler (slate-blue back).

Vocalizations. The song of the Prairie Warbler includes up to ten buzzy *zee-zee-zee* notes that go up in pitch. Male Prairie Warblers sing two variations of this song that vary in volume and speed of delivery. One song is to attract females, and the other is given to advertise the edges of the male's territory and is directed at other males.

Nesting. Prairie Warblers begin to arrive in our area in the spring as early as mid-April, although nesting activities don't typically begin until May. Males often return to their same territories year after year if the habitat is suitable. The nest is a cup made of plant fibers and lined with moss, grasses, fur, or feathers. The nest can be as high up as forty-five feet but is often placed less than ten feet above the ground. According to a study of about 750 Prairie Warbler nests in Indiana, the most common tree species used for nesting was the American elm. Prairie Warblers lay three to five whitish eggs that have brown speckles toward the end of the egg.

Matt Williams

39

Canada Warbler
(*Cardellina canadensis*)

STATUS:

2014 NABCI Yellow Watch List, 2016 NABCI
Watch List, 2016 PIF Watch List

ESTIMATED POPULATION TREND:

−65% during the period 1966–2015

LENGTH: 5–6"

Canada Warbler, June, Michigan: The male Canada Warbler has a yellow
breast, black necklace, bluish-gray back, and a distinct eye ring.

Breeding
Migration

Species Account. The Canada Warbler is one of those refreshing species of warbler that doesn't spend all of its time high above you lost in the treetops. On the breeding grounds, Canada Warblers forage within sixteen feet of the ground. During migration, the birds foraging heights ranged between five and twenty-three feet, with females tending to forage slightly closer to the ground than males. Canada Warblers will hover to glean prey from leaves, and they also catch insects on the wing—a habit that previously earned these birds the name "Canadian flycatcher." Many winged insects are taken, including mosquitoes, flies, and moths. Spiders and caterpillars also make up portions of the diet, as well as a few berries.

A well-named bird, over 80 percent of the Canada Warbler population nests in Canada, with the remainder nesting primarily in the northern tier of the eastern United States, including northern Michigan, Wisconsin, and Minnesota in the Midwest. A small number of birds nest in the Appalachian Mountains as far south as Georgia. The birds occur in cool, damp forest with a dense understory and mossy groundcover for nesting. Canada Warblers can be locally abundant in young forest (six to thirty years after disturbance) that can result from fire, timber harvests, or storms that blow down canopy trees. Interestingly, Canada Warblers tend to respond negatively to high deer populations, likely because of the loss of understory vegetation. A study from Massachusetts showed that in forests with one to three deer per approximately three square miles, eighty Canada Warblers were observed. In similar forests with thirteen to twenty-three deer per three square miles, only one Canada Warbler was observed.

The Canada Warbler is one of the later spring migrants and reaches peak numbers in the Midwest in the second or third week of May. It is also one of the first warblers to leave the breeding grounds in the fall as it makes its way to winter in Panama and northern South America, and it is usually gone from our region by early September. Disturbingly, results from Breeding Bird Survey routes indicate that the greatest declines in breeding populations of this bird are occurring in Canada, where the vast majority of the remaining population occurs. Some estimates are that the breeding population in Canada may have declined as much as 85 percent since 1968, with trends showing that the population decline is accelerating in recent years. In fact, according to BBS data, as much as 43 percent of the breeding population in Canada was lost in just the ten-year period from 1997 to 2007. These declines have led to the listing of this species as threatened in Canada. Habitat loss, especially on the wintering grounds in South America, is given as the primary reason for the decline. An estimated 95 percent of the cloud forest within the Canada Warbler's wintering range has been deforested since the 1970s. In Colombia alone, the rate of deforestation in the early 1990s is believed to have been between 1.5 and 2.2 million acres per year. This type of extreme habitat loss could well explain the steep declines of the Canada Warbler in recent decades. This species also seems susceptible to hitting obstructions while migrating at night. A remarkable 131 birds were killed in one night after colliding with a chimney in Ontario. In another case, twenty-seven Canada Warblers were killed when they collided with a television tower in Illinois.

Identification. The Canada Warbler is a beautiful bird with *slate-blue upperparts* and lemon yellow underparts with a whitish eye ring, yellow line from the beak to the eye, and *black "necklace" of short, vertical black streaks across its throat*. Males also have some black on the cheeks and small black streaks on the crown. Females are similarly patterned but less strikingly marked. The wings and tail of both sexes are unmarked. Simi-

lar species include the Magnolia Warbler, which in addition to a similar black necklace also has black streaking down the flanks and is black or olive on the back instead of the grayish blue of the Canada Warbler. The Kirtland's Warbler is also similar looking but has black streaks on the back and white wing bars that the Canada Warbler lacks.

Vocalizations. The song begins with a quick *chip* note and is followed by a short burst of rich, warbled notes that sound almost rushed or hurried. The song lasts only about two seconds in length.

Nesting. Canada Warblers lay three to five eggs that are creamy white and speckled with brown. Both parents care for the nestlings and feed them a diet of insects. The female builds the nest either on the ground or very close to it. The nest is usually placed in sphagnum hummocks or other mossy areas. Incubation lasts approximately twelve days, and chicks remain in the nest for an additional ten before fledging.

Matt Williams

Canada Warbler, May, Ohio: The female Canada is similar to the male but lacks the black on the crown and cheek, and has a less distinct necklace.

40 Wilson's Warbler
(*Cardellina pusilla*)

STATUS:

Common Bird in Steep Decline

ESTIMATED POPULATION TREND:

−61% during the period 1966–2015

LENGTH: 4.5"

Wilson's Warbler, June, Michigan: The adult male Wilson's Warbler has a glossy, jet-black cap with a bright-yellow face and throat.

Breeding
Migration
Nonbreeding

Species Account. Although this tiny warbler is often at or below eye level rather than in the tree tops, it can still be a frustrating bird to see well because it usually stays hidden in dense shrubs and is almost constantly in motion. Often, the best view of the bird is when it darts out to grab an insect on the wing or briefly hovers to snatch prey from a leaf before darting back into the underbrush. It was probably with this behavior in mind that Alexander Wilson first described the species in 1811 as the Green Black-capt Flycatcher. Whether they are fly catching or gleaning insects from vegetation while perched, Wilson's Warblers take a variety of prey, including flies, spiders, beetles, and caterpillars. In the winter, the birds have also been reported to feed on honeydew—a sweet, sticky substance produced by certain types of insects.

Wilson's Warblers are one of the most widespread species of warbler in the United States, with birds regularly occurring in every state except Hawaii. There are three subspecies recognized, with western birds averaging slightly larger and having a more gold-

Wilson's Warbler, June, Michigan: This bird shows more
olive coloration in the cap than the previous examples.
It is likely either a female bird or a young male.

en-yellow color than the eastern birds that we are familiar with here in the Midwest. Recent genetics testing indicates there may actually be six distinct breeding groups of Wilson's Warblers, with the birds that breed in eastern Canada and pass through the Midwest on migration primarily wintering on the Yucatán Peninsula in Mexico.

Eastern birds tend to nest in the boreal forest of Canada near bogs. Nests are placed on the ground, often in a depression at the base of a small shrub. Mosses, alders, and Labrador tea are species commonly reported in the general vicinity of nest sites. Farther west, nests are often found in wet meadow habitats near willows and shrubby cinquefoil. Unlike the majority of the population that places nests on the ground, Wilson's Warblers along the Pacific Coast construct their nests as high as five feet off the ground in shrubs.

Although Wilson's Warblers are very widespread and may still number as many as 60 million, records from the Breeding Bird Survey show an average decline of almost 2 percent per year, which is why the species was listed as a common bird in steep decline. The reasons for this decline remain somewhat unclear, although loss of riparian habitat, especially in the western United States, is a possible explanation. The birds have also been shown to decline following the use of phenoxy herbicides in Oregon, and numerous collisions with communications towers in Wisconsin and Minnesota have also been reported.

Endangered and Disappearing Birds of the Midwest

LIST OF CONTRIBUTORS

Francesca J. Cuthbert received her PhD in ecology at the University of Minnesota and is currently a professor in the Department of Fisheries, Wildlife and Conservation Biology, University of Minnesota–Twin Cities and a scientific investigator at the University of Michigan Biological Station. For the past thirty years her research has focused on three topics in avian biology and conservation: recovery of federal or state listed species (especially piping plovers); ecology and population dynamics of colonial nesting waterbirds; and ecology and management of abundant species (especially double-crested cormorants). Most of her research involves working closely with federal and state agency biologists to facilitate conservation and management in the Great Lakes region. She has advised more than forty MS and PhD students. Dr. Cuthbert is a past president of the Waterbird Society, member of the Waterbird Conservation Council of the Americas, and a fellow of the American Ornithological Society. In 2009 she was honored as a Recovery Champion by U.S. Fish and Wildlife Service for her career-long contributions to the conservation of the Great Lakes population of the Piping Plover.

Dave Ewert is an Avian conservation scientist with the Nature Conservancy. He works on several conservation topics, including winter habitat of the Kirtland's warbler in the Bahamas, protection of stopover sites for migratory birds in the Great Lakes region, and Great Lakes coastline and island protection. Dr. Ewert received his BS from the University of Michigan and his PhD from the City University of New York. His research and conservation projects have taken him to the West Indies, as well as Central and South America. He has served on boards of conservation organizations and teaches at the University of Michigan Biological Station.

Amy Kearns is assistant bird biologist for the State of Indiana Department of Natural Resources. She primarily works with surveying and monitoring Species of Greatest Conservation Need, including state-endangered Loggerhead Shrikes. In addition to conducting surveys to detect nesting and wintering shrikes, Amy also monitors nesting success, color bands individual shrikes, and speaks with landowners to encourage nesting habitat conservation. Amy has a BA from the University of Wisconsin–Madison and lives in southern Indiana with her family.

Richard Urbanek is a retired wildlife biologist of the U.S. Fish and Wildlife Service (FWS). He received BS and MA degrees from Southern Illinois University and a PhD from Ohio State University. As a research associate of the Ohio Cooperative Fish and Wildlife Research Unit, he specialized in crane ecology and reintroduction research programs based at Seney National Wildlife Refuge (NWR) in the Upper Peninsula of Michigan. He later served as refuge biologist at Seney until he transferred to Necedah NWR as FWS senior project biologist for the reintroduction of the eastern migratory Whooping Crane. Although he has worked on a wide variety of wildlife-related projects, his primary interest continues to be the Whooping Crane reintroduction, on which he continues to assist.

Matt Williams studied shorebirds at Manomet Observatory in Massachusetts and later helped operate a MAPS bird-banding station at Seney National Wildlife Refuge in the Upper Peninsula of Michigan. Matt began his career with The Nature Conservancy in 1997 conducting field research on the Fort Hood military base in central Texas and mapping nesting habitat for the federally endangered Golden-cheeked Warbler. Matt also spent three and a half years working with endangered Attwater's Prairie-Chickens in coastal Texas, where he helped manage releases of captive-bred birds, tracked released birds with radio telemetry, and led invasive species control and prescribed burn efforts to improve habitat for the birds. Matt is now director of conservation programs for The Nature Conservancy in Indiana, where he lives with his wife, Karyn, and their four children. More of Matt's photography can be seen at www.mattwilliamsnature photography.com.

ACQUISITIONS EDITOR   *Ashley Runyon*
PROJECT MANAGER   *David Miller*
BOOK & JACKET DESIGNER   *Pamela Rude*
COMPOSITION   *Tony Brewer*
TYPEFACES   *Arno, Bauer Bodoni*